RETRIEVAL & RENEWAL
Ressourcement
IN CATHOLIC THOUGHT

The middle years of this century marked a particularly intense time of crisis and change in European society. During this period (1930-1950), a broad intellectual and spiritual movement arose within the European Catholic community, largely in response to the secularism that lay at the core of the crisis. The movement drew inspiration from earlier theologians and philosophers such as Möhler, Newman, Gardeil, Rousselot, and Blondel, as well as from men of letters like Charles Péguy and Paul Claudel.

The group of academic theologians included in the movement extended into Belgium and Germany, in the work of men like Emile Mersch, Dom Odo Casel, Romano Guardini, and Karl Adam. But above all the theological activity during this period centered in France. Led principally by the Jesuits at Fourviére and the Dominicans at Le Saulchoir, the French revival included many of the greatest names in twentieth-century Catholic thought: Henri de Lubac, Jean Daniélou, Yves Congar, Marie-Dominique Chenu, Louis Bouyer, and, in association, Hans Urs von Balthasar.

It is not true — as subsequent folklore has it — that those theologians represented any sort of self-conscious "school": indeed, the differences among them, for example, between Fourviére and Saulchoir, were important. At the same time, most of them were united in the double conviction that theology had to speak to the present situation, and that the condition for doing so faithfully lay in a recovery of the Church's past. In other words, they saw clearly that the first step in what later came to be known as *aggiornamento* had to be *ressourcement* — a rediscovery of the riches of the whole of the Church's two-thousand-year tradition. According to de Lubac, for example, all of his own works as well as the entire *Sources chrétiennes* collection are based on the presupposition that "the renewal of Christian vitality is linked at least partially to a renewed exploration of the periods and of the works where the Christian tradition is expressed with particular intensity."

In sum, for the *ressourcement* theologians theology involved a "return to the sources" of Christian faith, for the purpose of drawing out the meaning and significance of these sources for the critical questions of our time. What these theologians sought was a spiritual and intellectual communion with Christianity in its most vital moments as transmitted to us in its classic texts, a communion which would nourish, invigorate, and rejuvenate twentieth-century Catholicism.

The *ressourcement* movement bore great fruit in the documents of the Second Vatican Council and has deeply influenced the work of Pope John Paul II and Cardinal Joseph Ratzinger, Prefect of the Sacred Congregation of the Doctrine of the Faith.

The present series is rooted in this twentieth-century renewal of theology, above all as the renewal is carried in the spirit of de Lubac and von Balthasar. In keeping with that spirit, the series understands *ressourcement* as revitalization: a return to the sources, for the purpose of developing a theology that will truly meet the challenges of our time. Some of the features of the series, then, will be:

- a return to classical (patristic-mediaeval) sources;
- a renewed interpretation of St. Thomas;
- a dialogue with the major movements and thinkers of the twentieth century, with particular attention to problems associated with the Enlightenment, modernity, liberalism.

The series will publish out-of-print or as yet untranslated studies by earlier authors associated with the *ressourcement* movement. The series also plans to publish works by contemporary authors sharing in the aim and spirit of this earlier movement. This will include interpretations of de Lubac and von Balthasar and, more generally, any works in theology, philosophy, history, literature, and the arts which give renewed expression to an authentic Catholic sensibility.

The editor of the Ressourcement series, David L. Schindler, is Gagnon Professor of Fundamental Theology at the John Paul II Institute in Washington, D.C., and editor of the North American edition of *Communio: International Catholic Review,* a federation of journals in thirteen countries founded in Europe in 1972 by Hans Urs von Balthasar, Jean Daniélou, Henri de Lubac, Joseph Ratzinger, and others.

The Heroic Face of Innocence

THREE STORIES
by
GEORGES BERNANOS

WILLIAM B. EERDMANS PUBLISHING COMPANY
GRAND RAPIDS, MICHIGAN

T&T CLARK
EDINBURGH

"Joan, Heretic and Saint" originally published as *Jeanne, relapse et sainte,* © 1934 by Librairie Plon, Paris; English translation by R. Batchelor first published as *Sanctity Will Out: An Essay on St. Joan,* © 1947 by Sheed and Ward, Inc., New York.

"Sermon of an Agnostic on the Feast of St. Thérèse" originally published in *Les Grands cimetières sous la lune,* © 1938 by Librairie Plon, Paris; English translation by Pamela Morris and David Louis Schindler, Jr., in *Communio* 24 (Fall 1997), © 1997 by *Communio: International Catholic Review.*

"Dialogues of the Carmelites" originally published as *Dialogues des Carmélites,* © 1949 by Le Seuil, Paris; English translation by Michael Legat first published as *The Fearless Heart,* © 1952 by The Newman Press, Westminster, Maryland.

This edition © 1999 Wm. B. Eerdmans Publishing Co.
Published jointly 1999 by
Wm. B. Eerdmans Publishing Co.
255 Jefferson Ave. S.E., Grand Rapids, Michigan 49503
and by
T&T Clark Ltd
59 George Street, Edinburgh EH2 2LQ Scotland

Printed in the United States of America

04 03 02 01 00 99   7 6 5 4 3 2 1

Library of Congress Cataloging-in-Publication Data

Bernanos, Georges, 1888-1948.
[Stories. English. 1999]
The heroic face of innocence: three stories by Georges Bernanos /
Georges Bernanos.
p.   cm.
Contents: Joan, heretic and saint / translated by R. Batchelor —
Sermon of an agnostic on the feast of St. Thérèse /
translated by Pamela Morris and David Louis Schindler, Jr. —
Dialogues of the Carmelites / translated by Michael Legat.
ISBN 0-8028-4565-7 (pbk.: alk. paper)
1. Bernanos, Georges, 1888-1948 — Translations into English.
I. Title.
PQ2603.E5875A23   1999
843'.912 — dc21   98-50872
                                                   CIP

British Library Cataloguing-in-Publication Data

A catalogue record for this book is available from the British Library

ISBN 0 567 08665 8

Contents

Foreword

GEORGES BERNANOS may not be a household name even for many educated English readers. But we venture to suggest that anyone with a thirst for truth would do well to listen to his voice, at once so tender and so forceful, anyone in particular with a thirst for qualities like fortitude, fidelity, innocence, and ardent charity — virtues so patronizingly dismissed nowadays as quaint but obsolete. Bernanos replies that when such virtues disappear, the child within us dies and our culture turns inevitably into a civilization of robots without a memory and of old men whose only passions are the calculations of the mind.

Before it had become fashionable in the Catholic Church to speak of the prophetic witness proper to the laity, this husband and father of a family, who struggled all his life as a life-insurance salesman to make ends meet, also produced "on the side" a dazzling array of novels, polemical essays, and other writings that will abide as one of the most *honorable* attempts by a Christian to come to terms in the area of literary creation and public discourse with the peculiar maladies and stunted hopes of our twentieth century.

The three selections we offer in this volume span the last twenty years of the life of Georges Bernanos (1888-1948), who is probably best known to the English-reading public for his profoundly moving novel, *The Diary of a Country Priest.* Perhaps no other modern writer has equaled Bernanos's success in portraying in thoroughly contemporary and dynamic works of literature the Christian mystery of redemption out of sin and death through self-sacrificial love. This alone is enough of a rarity in modern fiction to elicit our interest. But there is much more. At the beginning of his masterful study *Bernanos: An Ecclesial Existence,* the renowned theologian Hans Urs von Balthasar, intimately familiar with the whole of the Christian theological and cultural tradition, does not hesitate to say that "it could just be that in the great Catholic literary figures (Bloy, Péguy, Claudel, Bernanos) we find more originality and vibrancy of thought — an intellectual life thriving superbly in a free and open landscape — than we do in the somewhat broken-winded theology of our time, which is satisfied with quite slender fare." Thus, Balthasar seems to be saying, we go to someone like Georges Bernanos not only for the highest kind of aesthetic pleasure and illumination but indeed for the deepest kind of concrete Christian reflection and guidance.

The common theme that runs through our selections is reflected in the title of this volume: namely, Bernanos's deep conviction that what will save the world in the end is not intellectual achievement, or technological progress, or political effort, or genetic engineering, or theological acumen, but *the heroism of innocence.* In his view only the radical innocence of spiritual childhood can successfully undertake the feat of radically self-giving love, and no lasting transformation of either an individual heart or a whole society can come except as a result of such genuine love. It goes without saying that, for the ardent believer that Bernanos was, Christ is both the paragon and the source of such childlike boldness and daring innocence — Christ, the very foundation of whose divine person and power is his never being anything but the obedient Son of the eternal Father. In a world where everyone aspires to some form of spiritual patricide as prerequisite for self-affirmation, or at least to becoming a respectable CEO, Bernanos proposes that the way to genuinely fruitful heroism, sanctity, and joy is the way of radical interior childhood, which is to say the way of the gospel of Christ, where the Savior states categorically: "Unless you become like children, you will never enter the kingdom of heaven" (Matthew 18:3).

This common theme of heroic innocence and its redemptive promise is further enriched and nuanced by the fact that, in our three selections, Bernanos has chosen the figures of three very young women as embodiments of his reflections on the power of the vocation to Christian innocence.

Joan, Heretic and Saint dates from 1929, and from its first lines we catch the impulse of the author's admiration for Joan of Arc. Quoting at intervals from the actual minutes of the trial, Bernanos is able within a few pages to evoke the whole ecclesial and personal drama, with all its paradoxes and ironies. The essay is almost musical in its vibrancy of tone and sheer élan. The saint's youthful capacity to endure all forms of moral and physical outrage with a stout and joyful heart is set in counterpoint to the spiritual senility and desiccation of her judges and tormentors. Old men — scholastics and politicians — surround the visionary country girl like vampires feeding at her young and holy heart. "One can understand the security of these men," observes Bernanos. "What, after all, had they to fear?" Like the Pharisees of all times and places, Joan's judges were choking with their own religiosity. Their pious erudition had put them outside the possibility of ever being surprised by their own God: "Had He wished to speak to the dignitaries of the Church, He would have found some other mouthpiece than this young woman of strange tastes, with her hair cut round like a page's, her hose, her breeches, her high shoes, her short tunic, and her charming little divided cap. They were 'the sons of obedience, most humble religious who think like their masters, like their Ordinary.' She cried out: *'I look to my Judge, Who is the King of Heaven and earth! Yes, I look to the Creator of all things! I love Him with all my heart.'"*

And Bernanos concludes this essay by sounding the flourish of one of his most original themes, of which Joan of Arc's life and destiny becomes an emblem: "Let others look to the spiritual side of things, argue about it, legislate about it; it is the temporal that we hold in both hands: we hold in both hands the temporal Kingdom of God. We hold the temporal heritage of the saints. For there were blessed along with us the corn and the wine, the stone of our thresholds and the roof where the dove builds her nest. . . ." Not materialism, but a bourgeois spiritualism that neatly pushes God back into His heaven and domesticates the impetus of grace is what Bernanos identifies as the rot eating away at the Christian soul in our century. No wonder, he muses, that the vitality of the younger generations often finds this version of Christianity a deadly bore!

The second selection, "Sermon of an Agnostic on the Feast of St. Thérèse," is really only an excerpt from a much longer work, *The Great*

Cemeteries under the Moon, published in 1938 in the context of the Spanish Civil War. This fictional sermon is Bernanos at his imaginative best, the deeply believing Catholic looking at a typical church-going congregation through the eyes of an unbeliever who on this occasion is allowed to climb the pulpit. Balthasar comments that the sermon "is no fervorino, but rather one of the most beautiful in all of modern homiletic literature, and in any event the most impressive and useful. The unbeliever holds a mirror up to the pious congregation, in which it can see how the world sees it from the outside and what the world has with perfect right expected from it but which they have never delivered." At the climax of his sermon, the agnostic paradoxically speaks words which in our day only the rarest priest dares to utter: "It is you, Christians, who participate in divinity as your liturgy proclaims; it is you, 'divine men,' who ever since His Ascension have been His representatives on earth. Well, you must admit that one would hardly know it at first glance! . . . Your only way out is to become children yourselves, to rediscover the heart of childhood. . . . In speaking thus, I don't think I am betraying the inspiration of Saint Thérèse of Lisieux. I am simply interpreting it. I am trying to turn it to some human use in the affairs of the world. . . . Christians, hurry up and become children again, that we [unbelievers] may become children too. It can't be so very difficult. Because you do not live your faith, your faith has ceased to be a living thing. It has become abstract — bodiless. Perhaps we shall find that the disincarnation of the Word of God is the real cause of all our misfortune."

The final and longer selection, *Dialogues of the Carmelites,* dating from 1948, the last year of Bernanos's life, may indeed emerge as his literary and religious masterpiece. The idea for this dramatic scenario came to Bernanos from another great Catholic writer of this century, the German poet and novelist Gertrud von le Fort. The plot and many of the characters are based on the actual historical event of the imprisonment and execution in 1794 of the sixteen nuns of the Carmel at Compiègne during the Reign of Terror. Bernanos's work is the basis for the inspiration and the libretto of Francis Poulenc's famous opera *Les Dialogues des Carmélites.* Although the work admirably evokes the frenetic atmosphere of the French Revolution and the massive crisis into which it plunged the whole of French society, the real strength of Bernanos's text is the manner in which it is able to explore the souls and hearts of a small number of characters in the face of the horror daily coming closer. The central character is the young novice, Blanche de la Force, in fact a fictional creation of Bernanos's whose spiritual path is symbolized by her name: the triumphant aristocratic surname "de la Force" yields to Blanche's new identity, expressed in the name she chooses in religious life, "Blanche of the Agony of Christ," and this change in name indeed announces her entering interiorly into the Passion of the Savior, shared in her own soul. The scaffold enthroning the guillotine becomes for Blanche and her sister nuns their personal embodiments of Golgotha.

In *Dialogues of the Carmelites,* a work so mature, moving, and thematically exhaustive that it can stand as a summation of all his works, Bernanos shows himself a master interweaving most deftly the psychological, historical, and religious dimensions of human experience in the middle of catastrophic social upheaval. And yet this alone would not stamp upon his creation the impact and originality it possesses, for these come from what must be termed the properly theological element. At the heart of all his reflections, denunciations, characterizations, and lyrical effusions, what we find in Georges Bernanos is a consuming zeal to show the world the overwhelming truth of the Pauline doctrine of the triumph of God's grace and power through all the rebelliousness and weakness of man: "The foolishness of God is wiser than men, and the weakness of God is stronger than men. . . . God chose what is foolish in the world to shame the wise, God chose what is weak in the world to shame the strong, God chose what is low and despised in the world, even things that are not, to bring to nothing things that are, so that no human being might boast in the presence of God. He is the source of your life in Christ Jesus, whom God made our wisdom, our righteousness and sanctification and redemption; therefore, as it is written, 'Let him who boasts, boast of the Lord' " (1 Corinthians 1:25, 27-31).

July 25, 1998
Feast of St. James the Apostle

Erasmo Leiva-Merikakis
University of San Francisco

Joan, Heretic and Saint

TRANSLATED BY R. BATCHELOR

EVER SINCE our dear Péguy went to his end, walking through the thick dust of summer, with his checked handkerchief over the nape of his neck, and his stout shoes taking great strides along the highway; ever since then, one would have liked Joan of Arc to belong only to children. In any case, everything, if they will take it, does belong to them from now onwards, for the hands of the old are too nerveless to hold the world. But alas, no one realizes it. The divine opportunity will be lost like so many others; the vice-like clutch, which relaxed for one moment, will close on us again tomorrow. The old man, with his feeble grip and his tireless jaw-muscles, will again start mumbling between his gums the lie that is as stale as his breath. On one day only — one single day out of all those we have lived — on November the eleventh of a bygone year, he stopped mumbling for a moment, and listened. The bells had been ringing themselves almost out of their belfries across the dreary November day; they had been skipping, like rams, knocking their vast heads one against the other; then, with a stamp of their steel hooves, escaping to the four corners of the earth. The glum sky of November echoed with their terrible frolics. Even the guns were hushed. They squatted in countless thousands on their enormous haunches, still warm from the last shell, their slender black heads turned upwards, scanning the clouds with their single eye. It was then that the old man felt himself alone — really alone for the first time; alone among so many of the young dead; intolerably alone in a world drained of color. "Is the heart still beating?" he asked. But the world's heart is always beating.

1

That heart is childhood. Were it not for the sweet scandal of childhood, avarice and cunning would have dried up the world in a century or so. Our poor planet, for all its chemists and its engineers, would be only a whitened bone hurled through space. But the spirit of old age, which sets out patiently to conquer the world, always loses at the last moment; then starts afresh, to lose once more: untiring, inexorable. It is the spider weaving and reweaving his Cartesian philosophy, in which a drop of dew trembles at dawn. Just when the old man raises a finger to set a thousand typists in action, just when the peace of the world is about to emerge from all this machinery, in comes a young girl, mocking and tender, who belongs to no one, and whose soft voice answers the political theologians with old sayings and proverbs, after the manner of shepherds. The democratic Abbés of the illustrious University of Paris, with their dream of some sort of universal republic; the distinguished pacifist prelates, dazzled by the dollar rate and impressed by the solidity of the good Burgundian coins; the Carmelite Eustache, making up to the Communist flayers of the Butchers' Corporation; the graduates of the Rue Clos-Bruneau; the clerics of the Rouen Chapter and those of the Chapter of M. Julien Benda — all these old men, many of them under thirty, look enviously at this little France who is so fresh, so mischievous, who is awfully afraid of being burnt, but still more afraid of telling a lie. "Just overlook it!" she says. "Spare me." She finds it very hard not to laugh when this member "of the higher clergy, a most prudent and benign personage," His Grace the Strictly Concordatory Bishop of Beauvais, sets out to prove that she does not like the people of Burgundy. "Ah, those Burgundians! So well-disciplined, so pious, so rich! Ah, the Burgundian methods! Has the accused ever seen a Burgundian close to — seen, really *seen* one?" "You bet I have," says Joan. "There was one at Domrémy, and I should have liked someone to cut his head off — I mean, of course, if it had pleased God." Poor, poor little Joan, who only said this out of mischief, for the pleasure of seeing all these drowsy faces lose their gravity. "Get along with you! I know all about your Burgundians!" They shift on their seats, make a sign to the recording clerks, blow out their cheeks, and murmur like cats. Sometimes one of them drops off to sleep and his chin hits the desk; or he gives a slight belch, which he corrects gravely, with an ecclesiastical hand. Then the silence begins again, and the boredom. She again hears the rustling of the parchments, the scratching of the pens, the breathing of these overfed, somnolent men. Good Lord, yes, she's very afraid of the fire, but she can't help shrugging her shoulders, yawning, saying "Thank you for telling me," or "Believe me or not just as you like," or, with a shake of her proud little head, "People are often hanged for having told the truth." . . . But all the time she is thinking: "If I could only come here with ten of my men, you wouldn't look too happy." And when she is led away, worn out with exhausted nerves, with fatigue, with a kind of childish disgust, she cries out: "You're really taking a lot on yourselves, and you're putting too much on me!" She is red with anger, and her eyes are full of tears.

THE MARVEL IS that once, and perhaps only once in the history of the world, childhood stood thus before a regular tribunal; but the marvel above all others is that this tribunal should have been a tribunal of the Church. And it was no joke. We must recognize quite frankly that no one was ever more respectful of the letter of the law, more careful to avoid what today we should call the Court of Appeal, more skilful at setting the vast machinery of procedure in motion, and guiding its actions. For the legend of a scamped inquiry and a judgment unjustified in law cannot survive a reading of the texts, and could never deceive anyone but an innocent schoolgirl. To any unbiased mind, it is quite enough to quote Brother Jean le Maître, representing Brother Jean Graverent, the Inquisitor for heretical perversity and Delegate of the Holy See throughout the realm of France; the august Chapter of Rouen and the Official of the same city; Monsignor Gilles; the Abbot of Fécamp; the Archdeacon of Eu; the Archdeacon of Evreux; His Grace the Bishop of Coutances; His Grace the Bishop of Lisieux; His Grace the Bishop of Thérouanne; His Grace the Bishop of Noyon; the Reverend Abbot of Jumièges; the Reverend Abbot of Cormeilles; and fifty-three Doctors, Graduates, or Bachelors of Arts — that is to say, the illustrious University of Paris, and more especially the Theological Faculty. The Popes themselves feared this Faculty; it was the sovereign arbiter of kings, made up as it was of almost all the eminent theologians, Regulars of every Order, and Seculars of every nation, whom the Christendom of that day could boast. *The foremost men that are on earth,*" as Jouvenal des Ursins was to say later, *"for not only are the King and his Realm thereby informed of the truth of the Faith but all*

Christendom too." They were men of the Council, who had deposed three Popes, and who twenty years later were to depose that very Eugene IV who had paid fatherly tribute to the fair fame of Pierre Cauchon, years after Joan's death, when he transferred him to the See of Lisieux. He had praised, moreover, the holy teachings of the Masters of the University of Paris, *"their zeal in preserving the purity of that light which shines forth in the house of the Lord — the river which flows from the springs of Wisdom."* It is useless for us to try, with over-subtle distinctions, to turn this regular and duly-constituted tribunal into something that was quite out of order — a sort of tragic farce. One fact alone should put an end to these feeble attempts — the fact that the Holy Inquisition itself intervened in the trial, and that the seal of the Apostolic Delegate was set beside that of the Bishop of Beauvais at the foot of the iniquitous judgment. A year before, it was in the following terms that the Vicar General of the Inquisitor of the Faith in the Realm of France had accused the poor child to the Duke of Burgundy:

"Using the rights of our office and the authority committed to us by the Holy See in Rome, under pain of law we require of and enjoin on every person of whatsoever state, condition, preeminence and authority, to bring before us as a prisoner the above-named Joan, that she may appear before us against the Procurator of the Holy Inquisition, and to reply and proceed, as is fitting, to the good counsel, favor, and aid of the good doctors and masters of the University of Paris, and other notable counsellors."[1]

What more is needed? There remained, no doubt, an appeal to the Pope. But to begin with it is not true that such an appeal was a matter of right; and it would be too foolish or too dishonest to use it as an argument against so strongly grounded a judgment, when the *Directorium Inquisitorum* sets forth as an incontestable principle that the Inquisitor acts as a delegate of the Pope, even when he is appointed by the priests of his Order. Who, moreover, can fail to see that on these lines we should be in danger of annulling any judgment whatever of the Holy Inquisition, to say nothing of the endless trials for heresy instigated by the Ordinaries according to Canon Law? Can one claim, in sheer desperation, that the

---

1. Jouvenal des Orsins, quoted by Champion in his excellent book, *Le Procès de Condemnation de Jeanne D'Arc,* which has been so largely drawn on here.

Chief Inquisitor himself had been bought by the English? It would at least appear that his contemporaries had no suspicion of it. On the contrary, what amazes us, and what by itself is enough to convince us of the authentic character of the judgment pronounced at Rouen, is the general silence which followed its promulgation. Until the beginning of the Process of Rehabilitation — that is, until the day when the King of France made his power sufficiently felt — it is impossible to discover a single written testimony, or even the record of a single verbal witness, in favor of the little saint who had been dishonored, convicted of witchcraft, and branded with the terrible sign. Even during the first discussion, with a defensive movement which reflects more credit on his political sense than on his clear-sightedness or his courage, the Archbishop of Rheims — the same Archbishop who had anointed the Dauphin, seen Joan with his own eyes, and touched her loyal hand with his own — warned his flock against the witless girl who always insisted on going her own way against all wiser heads, and whose pretended miracles were mere vulgar delusions. "The little shepherd of the Gévaudan can do better," added the wise prelate. What is more — so infamous was the suspicion which from that time she felt weighing on her that the poor child showed no anxiety at all to see the witnesses of the French party appear at Rouen — the Boussacs, the Bourdons, the de la Trémoilles and the La Hires, who but yesterday had been her companions, and to whom the Tribunal was willing to offer guarantees of safe-conduct. *I would rather write to them about the whole trial,* said she.

It is no doubt true that a certain number of her judges made no secret of their English or Burgundian sympathies, but there was nothing in this to scandalize anybody, since the principle of submission to recognized authority, whatever the origin of this authority, has never been seriously questioned by the holders of benefices. "When it comes to blows, we shall see who has the better right to the God of Heaven," said poor Joan. It was a childish taunt, as much out of place at the tribunal in Rouen as it would be today at Locarno, or uttered before the statisticians and professors of international law at Geneva. It would be as vain to reproach the judges of Rouen and Paris for their loyalty to Henry VI — the son of that Henry V whose piety and reverence towards the Apostolic See had so greatly edified the Christian world — as it would be to reproach

Pope Pius VII for having hastened to Notre Dame, over the bodies of so many martyrs, to crown a Second Lieutenant of Artillery King of France. There is no real spirit of peace without a strong dose of opportunism. Should we not rather admire the fact that this illustrious tribunal — which was a kind of University Holy Synod, drunk with spiritual power and convinced that it was the source from which all legitimacy proceeded — should have convoked so many "scientific and learned persons" for the sole purpose of discussing a case of conscience with an illiterate little peasant girl? If we can compare an over-modest scientific society with the University of the fifteenth century, can we imagine the Academy of Medicine filling page after page with reports, formulating seventy titles of accusation, and holding a great number of solemn meetings, to judge the case of some bone-setting shepherd with healing powers? It is true that after a lapse of five centuries we could wish that Joan had been spared so long, so tortuous, and so eloquent an agony; we would rather she had been devoured by wolves than nibbled by these foxes of the Schools — these rats. Nevertheless, assuming that one accepts the lawfulness of the Church's jurisdiction, can one reproach her for carrying out a trial according to her own methods, by argument? Could one hope to bring a conviction for heresy as easily as for a quarrel after a few drinks, or for a theft of rabbits? But what (one may ask) had these Church dignitaries to do with a little shepherdess? To begin with, this little shepherdess claimed to be in communication with Heaven. That she was in communication with the spirits was quite possible; let her leave it to prudent and learned people to decide whether these spirits were good or bad. This was expressed by sixteen Doctors and six Licentiate Members or Bachelors of the Theological Faculty, who declared: *"By asserting, as firmly as she holds the Christian faith, that these apparitions were St. Michael, St. Catherine, and St. Margaret, and that their words and acts were good, the said woman must be held suspect of erring in faith; for if she holds that the articles of faith are no more certain than her own beliefs, then she errs in faith."* And Denis Gastinet, a Member of the Faculty, wrote: *"She considers herself an authority, a doctor, a master, while being in reality a flagrantly mistaken person, a schismatic, a heretic!"* The grimace of this scornful theologian comes down to us across five centuries — five centuries, or perhaps across some other abyss where there are no eyes or ears?

6

Of course such words are hard; today they sound impious. But at the time when they were spoken they do not seem to have shocked many people. At any rate, they were received in silence for more than twenty years. It was an almost unbroken silence, and not only in English territory. For Joan's judges lived out their days full of honors and loaded with benefices. Jean Beaupère, the Rector of the University, went to live at Besançon under the protection of the King of France. Thomas de Courcelles, who had recommended that the poor child should be tortured *"for a medicine to her soul,"* was to die as the dean of the Chapter House of Notre Dame; another of her judges, Guillaume de Conti, welcomed Charles VII on his solemn entry into the good city of Paris. Thomas Loiseleur finished his career peacefully at Basel, and it is not true that he was ever banished. Pierre Cauchon represented the English Church at the Council of 1435, and died at his magnificent house, Saint-Cande, at Rouen, in the arms of his barber. Cardinal Beaufort, who had been at one time the Legate of Pope Martin V in Germany, and who had preached the Crusade against the Hussites, was to end up as Chancellor of England. Philibert, the Bishop of Coutances, was to spend three years in Bohemia working for the reunion of that country with the Church; he then left his See to Gilles de Duremort, another of the Maid's assassins. Zanon, the Bishop of Lisieux, was to rally to King Charles VII, when the cause of Henry VI seemed too greatly compromised. He was appointed Bishop of Pavia in 1453, represented Pope Calixtus III at the Council of Ratisbonne, received the Cardinal's hat in 1456, and died as Legate of the Marches of Ancona, through the good graces of Pope Pius II. As for the celebrated John, Duke of Bedford, who was perhaps the one hyena among all these foxes and rats, he became Canon of Rouen through the help of the Carmelites, to whom he showed every favor in his power; he lies today, surrounded by his pious brethren, in the choir of the Cathedral.

One can understand the security of these men. What, after all, had they to fear? Among all the witches and sorcerers whom the Inquisitor's axe uprooted every year, there stood one little girl, highly suspect, with her bright fearless eyes and her man's dress, and her claim to go back to the reverend Fathers in God. The axe cut her down with the rest. If she wanted to save her life, she had only to recant, to abjure these idle phantoms — against the evidence of her own senses, if need be, since docility

7

is always better than presumption. *"Item, in conclusion, the said woman was once again strongly admonished to submit to the Church, on pain of being abandoned by the Church. Who, if the Church abandoned her, would be in great danger of fire, both temporal and eternal."* To this she replied with a cry of distress — a child's dear cry, whose flight through the air one would like to kiss; a cry of appeal which would have brought the sword of any knight leaping from its scabbard; the cry of innocence which from age to age would be answered by the furious thunder of the French guns — "You shall never do to me what you say without bringing harm on yourselves, both soul and body."

But what weight had one defiance more or less in the delicately adjusted scales of the judges? A hundred times, a thousand times, they had heard the same puerile threat, and they had never yet seen God's thunderbolt strike the table round which they were deliberating — falling between the Dictionary of Canon Law and the *Directorium Inquisitorum*. Besides, they would have regarded so unworthy a fear as blasphemous, sacrilegious, and a piece of pure superstition: God does not thunder against His own judgments. Had He wished to speak to the dignitaries of the Church, He would have found some other mouthpiece than this young woman of strange tastes, with her hair cut round like a page's, her hose, her breeches, her high shoes, her short tunic, and her charming little divided cap. They were "the sons of obedience, most humble religious who think like their masters, like their Ordinary." She cried out: *"I look to my Judge, Who is the King of Heaven and earth! Yes, I look to the Creator of all things! I love Him with all my heart."* "First love and honor the Church," they replied. "And above all, don't go in for politics."

It is quite obvious that the thought of politics obsessed these solid scholastic heads, and not, as one might think, out of temporal motives alone. The rebirth of nationalism, the old prejudices of countries which were beginning to set up rival princes, all this seemed to them infinitely more to be feared than any feudal quarrels, which they had always been able to put a stop to by arbitration. They were the masters of an invisible world which was forever overstepping the boundaries of the visible and absorbing it; they were the sovereign law-givers, the one repository of all knowledge; they communicated with one another in the same universal tongue. Moreover, they were the only aristocracy that owed nothing to he-

redity. As though freed from all carnal ties to be the wonder and admiration of the sturdy barons, they felt themselves strong enough to make any
concessions of fact to the temporal powers; but it outraged them to compromise their prestige in a matter of national conscience.

"On Saturday the 24th of February she said that she came from God,
and that she had nothing to do with this trial, and asked to be sent back to
God, from Whom she had come. Item, on Saturday the 17th of March she said
that God had sent her to succor the realm of France." Joan's story is today so
familiar that such words have no longer power to move us: they have become legendary. They are not now even of yesterday. Yet one wonders
what welcome tomorrow will have for them. "Item, the said Joan, usurping
to herself the office of the angels, said and affirmed that she was sent by God,
even in what concerns violence and the shedding of human blood. Which is
entirely contrary to sanctity, and hateful and abominable to all pious minds."
To this, it is true, the poor child replied that, in the first place, she had
asked for peace to be made; but if they would not make peace, then she
was ready to fight. That, indeed, is the pacifism of fighting people, for
there are certainly not many cases of generals who insist on taking by
force what others are prepared to give them of their own free will. There
are certain pious folk of the tearful species, whom the least act of political
violence drives to frenzy — a frenzy of streaming eyes and protruding
tongues. They pay homage in the shops round St. Sulpice to the plaster
Joans in cuirasses of painted aluminum, and pretend not to know that
some of those very Englishmen who came to peer at the Maid through
the grating of the Vieux-Marché had once seen her enter the fortress of
Saint Loup, her banner held high and her armor streaming with blood.

O sacred face! O dear face of my country, O fearless eyes! They saw
your poor cheeks hollowed by fever, the sweat standing out on your stub-
born little forehead, and the quivering of your mouth, when you who for
so many days had been hemmed in by your enemies in the stifling air of
the courtroom, suddenly refused to stand up to them — when you took
back your word and your oath, O flower of chivalry! They thought that
for one moment, for just one moment, they had seen French honor in
danger — your own dear honor, as fresh as a lily. So they left us nothing
of you but this lifeless and harmless image, this chocolate-box picture, to
be the dream of the seminaries. Did they burn her, or just refuse to admit

her to the examinations of the advanced catechism class? They surrounded the martyr with a rampart of stomachs, of fat thighs, of bald skulls polished like ivory; but right at the back, over their heads, she caught a glimpse of open sky, the harsh and windy sky of March which favors long night rides, and ambushes, and fine feats of arms. She was thinking: "La Hire, perhaps? Or the dear Prince of Alençon?" *"On Thursday the first of March, she said that the English would have greater losses than they had ever had yet. When questioned whether this would take place before the Feast of St. Martin in the winter, she replied that before that time they would see many things, and it was possible that the English would be overthrown and brought to the earth. When asked what were the great danger and peril which we, the Bishops and other clerics, incurred by bringing her to trial, she replied that she would receive help: that she did not know whether she would be delivered from prison, or whether some disaster might not take place, and she thought that it would be for a great victory."*

Let us for a moment think over those sacred words. Blessed were you, Bishop and Count of Beauvais, Councillors, Apostolic and Imperial Notaries and Doctors — blessed were you to hear them from such lips, in the open court, in that lifeless atmosphere, reeking with boredom, envy, and hair-splitting hatred — to hear these words of victory, these childish words, these words of eternal childhood, like an armful of roses torn from the heart of night and drenched with the last shower, sweet with their wild fragrance. They were too human for you, too living, they hurt you too cruelly. You suddenly heard the sword ring in the scales; from the North Sea to the banks of the Jordan, you heard the old chivalry stirring under the earth. There was not one of those fair-moustached giants, forever rusted into his armor, who would not have recognized one of his own race. At every window and every door of the vast hall where the injustice was being consummated, there should, in a flash, have appeared one of these men — secret, impenetrable, invulnerable, with the bronze mace in his right hand, and in his left the shield with its mouth of steel. *"Item, the said Joan caused to have painted her coat-of-arms, in which she set two lilies or in a field azure, and in the heart of the lilies, a sword argent with handle and cross or, which would seem to pertain to vanity, not to piety or religion, for to attribute such vanities to God is to run contrary to the reverence due to God and the angels."* Then Brother Inquisitor Jean le Maître rose

10

up, and denounced the sword, the azure, the lilies, and the honor of knighthood.

But as the end of the trial approached, and the tormented saint, driven hour by hour through her guileless and fragile defense, began to weaken, one suddenly feels an unexpected pity for her judges. At the point which they had now reached, no human power could have drawn them back; they were carried down by their own weight; they fell like stones. As long as they seemed to be fighting foot by foot, piling up proofs, doing their work as judges and as pedants, risking their tonsures in the debate, so long did they inspire more fear than shame. But now they abandoned the attempt to teach theology to a girl of twenty, and broke off the ludicrous juggling with words, not of their own wish, but because Joan had just put herself in their hands, and they didn't know what to do with her. The machine had been set going too carefully, and was now out of the engineers' control. Quite suddenly, the evidence overwhelmed both victim and judges.

Besides, they had already given their reasons, supplied their texts, paraphrased, quoted; they were squeezed dry, just as a surgeon slips his hands out of his gloves, tears off his mask, and drinks down the first draught of air, so too was their task accomplished, and they looked, with a kind of terrible, weary solicitude, at the little victim who had been so skillfully made ready. The time had come now for them to pity themselves and the fragile object of their labors: to let their old, contracted hearts expand. For many of them were old men, attached to their homes, to their table, to their servants, and impatient to take up the thread of their peaceful lives: the first warm days of spring were making them conscious of their livers. The case was settled: it was time to have done with it. And also, was it quite fitting work for Canons and Professors and learned men — this *tête-à-tête*, dragging on for so many days, with a pretty girl dressed in man's clothes; this murmur of the studious classroom, the low hum of references quoted from desk to desk, and suddenly, the voice of a young woman breaking in? The unending dispute, no longer over texts, but carried on in front of the fresh young body destined for the flames, must end by seeming suspect to the best of them: must trouble their consciences. Did not one of them remark one day that according to the testimony of the Fathers the devil could take on an angelic form? Was he, or was he not, thinking of Joan? Twenty years later, another judge, Jean Beaupère, an outstanding man who had once been Rector of the University, when questioned during the preliminaries of the Process of Rehabilitation, was to say that the Maid had made fools of the Churchmen, and that she was most dangerously *"subtle, with the subtlety proper to women."* That was all they could get out of him.

Subtle or not, on Wednesday, the twenty-third of March, the little victim was ready, bound most skillfully, without any violence, by those expert, careful hands: clerkly hands that were almost maternal. She was ready for the executioner, for she had said all she knew — all that needed to be known. And so, rejected as she was by God — *a scandal, a blasphemer, an apostate* — and robbed of her soul, they watched her as she stirred humbly, in the depth of her great misery. For three months they had been patiently teaching her theology, the Scriptures, and the Fathers, and she now knew enough — she knew too much — to hope to be right against them all; and anyway, what good would it do her to be right? She was accursed. The soldiers who had once asked her for charms and who had wanted to tell her their dreams; the heads of the army who, after a cup or two, would nudge each other and laugh as she went by; the high dignitaries of the Church whose over-sharp eyes she could hardly bear; the starveling, fanatical monks; the rough-tongued preachers who saw devils everywhere and who did not much believe in the virtue of girls; the mincing fine ladies, with that disconcerting little movement of the chin and that flash of their blue eyes; all that enchanted world through which she had moved as if it were a dream, and where she herself had been but a dream — it was all passing forever, fading away. If by some miracle she could one day go back to it, the frightful shadow of sorcery, of traffic with unclean spirits, would follow her. Even if she could be rescued from her judges, and free, no priest who knew her past would ever, without a shudder, raise his consecrated hand to give her absolution. . . . But she would never go back; she would not find her own people there. Even now, if anyone there spoke of her, he would sigh and shake his head. The knowing ones would murmur: "I told you so. Is the King going to risk a quarrel with the Churchmen for the sake of a shepherdess? It's a stupid and an ugly business." Even, alas, her old mother . . . So many Bishops, mitred Abbots, holy religious, doctors of the Sorbonne, all assembled to judge her little girl, her little Joan. After all, dear God, can one be sure? So why should one leave one's own part of the world, set out on the roads — ah, poor wretch! But Isabeau Romée-Zabilet in her own *patois* — was not one to tell her troubles to others: she shut her thin lips over them, and looked everyone straight in the face with her unflinching eyes. One just has to swallow it down and bear it somehow. The King . . . the King met her sometimes, and took her hand sadly; then he went away. She had already summed him up, just as she would have summed up a son or daughter-in-law, with one shrewd, empirical glance. He was a melancholy young man, indolent and secretive, eaten up with remorse and scruples, who for ten years now had lived hidden *"in castles, mean dwellings, and all manner of small chambers."* He had been kept in the paths of human prudence and the fear of hell by his intimate adviser, the Archbishop of Rheims, Renault de Chartres, who wanted peace with the Burgundians and who publicly mocked at the Maid's so-called mission. It was not until he was on the threshold of old age that Charles VII was to learn what pleasure was, and to enjoy wine and women: at that time, he was still doubtful about his birth, his right, his friends, his enemies; he was doubtful about everything, and sought comfort in his devotions. Being the son of such a mother, and having been shy and precocious as a child, he had never really lived, save on that day, that one day, when the intrepid young girl had come to him, pushing her way through the great hall with her two bare proud little hands: she was pale, pale as death, with a set jaw. And now Joan was asking herself: "What will he think? What is the Bishop of Orleans thinking?" "God loves them a hundred times more dearly than me; my saints have told me so!" she exclaimed on three occasions before her astounded judges, who at once seized their pens and indited: *"Item, you said, Joan, that you knew well that God loves certain living persons better than yourself, and that you had learnt this by a revelation from St. Catherine and St. Margaret. As to this article, the clerks say that therein lies a temerarious and presumptuous assertion, a superstitious divination, and a blasphemy against the saints."* "No matter what I do," thought the poor child, "they will still ask themselves: 'Was she not one of those girls who practice enchantments and witches' Sabbaths, who give their bodies to the demon, who renounce all modesty, and who deceive their followers right to the end?'" Oh, the ghastly thought!

13

And so everything failed the marvellous girl in her agony. From week to week, from day to day, from hour to hour, the interrogation — which there has been a silly attempt to represent as a miraculous duel of eloquence in which Joan always had the last word — slowly tore her from herself, uprooted her. Ah, you saw her eyes slowly fill with shadows, and when you appeared on the threshold, you saw her first movement of retreat towards the wall, and the artless self-defense of her little lowered head. There were eight of them, on that Wednesday of May the twenty-third, eight men between her and the day — the narrow window with its corner of blue sky, the innocent sky of May. Eight men, eight peaceable clerks facing her who had so often spurred her horse against the long fifteen-foot pikes, with cries and oaths all round her, and the cords of the cross-bows ringing in her ears, and the arrows rattling against her cuirasse. Master Pierre Maurice, the Canon of the church at Rouen, read the text of the schedule: *"Item, you said . . . Item, you said . . . As to this article, the clerks said . . ."* Twelve times did Joan avoid his eyes, and when his met hers by chance he lowered them at once and gave a little cough. Was she thinking of the little church in Lorraine, of her parish? Was it not her own village priest who was just about to drive her from her bench before he sang High Mass, and who would shut the church door against her with the same old hand which had so often given her Communion? *"As to these articles, the clerks say you are a schismatic, with wrong notions of the unity and authority of the Church, and even until today erring perniciously in your faith."* But those were words she had heard too often; they had become so familiar, so monotonous, that they hardly caused her any feeling now except boredom. They bored her. She looked furtively out of the window, counted the beams in the ceiling, and sighed, like an absent-minded schoolgirl. . . . Oh, Lord! Whom did her lovely horses belong to now — first of all her seven saddle-horses with their plaited manes and their tied-up tails; then the five chargers, fat with corn and shining — twelve fine beasts they were! What with grooms, pages, sergeants, chaplains, it was true that she had had the retinue of a great lord. How fast her heart used to beat when all those horsemen rode behind her with a sound of thunder! She had not feared blows, or death, or any living soul; she would have led her Frenchmen anywhere; she would have charged against a hundred men! Sometimes a mendicant friar with bare feet and filthy hair

would shrug his shoulders or spit in the dust as she went by; or elderly ladies, at the halting stage, would screw up their mouths at the sight of her
fine surcoat falling below the knee. *"Item, you arrayed yourself in sumptuous garments, in precious stuffs, and in furs. You used long tabards and divided skirts. It is notorious that when captured you were wearing under your
coat-of-mail a tunic of cloth-of-gold."* What had it to do with these preachers — these false preachers? Would they even have been able to tell a surcoat from a hauberk, or a festooned cap from an ordinary cap with a cockade? She had loved the horses, the rides in single file, the parades, the
starry nights of bivouac, the slow approaches down hollow lanes between
high grassy banks, the coming out on the plateau, the rattling of a hundred banners, the snorting of the horses, and the town that was to be
taken lying blue below them. She had loved the things that soldiers love,
and loved them as soldiers love them; never getting attached to anything,
ready each day to leave everything, and coming up to get their daily bread
from the hand of God. What was the good now of reproaching her with
having thrown money to the wind? The king had filled her coffers, and
anyone who liked had helped himself. That was the way God had made
soldiers. What soldier has ever grown rich and miserly? It is enough that
they should live and die like the little children who resemble them.

Master Pierre Maurice finished his reading, laid his roll of parchment on the table, and wiped his forehead. The others drew near. There
in that narrow room were the Bishops of Thérouanne and of Noyon,
Master Jean de Châtillon, the Archdeacon of Evreux, Jean Beaupère,
Nicholas Midi, Guillaume Erart, André Marguerie and Nicolas de
Venderès, Archdeacons or Canons of the church of Rouen. For the first
time, perhaps, Joan exchanged with them — with her judges — a look of
despairing helplessness: a look of farewell. They no longer belonged to
the world: they were growing further and further away from her, vanish-
ing with a terrible swiftness. "Do not leave us alone, Joan!" screamed the
appalled old men. "Do not cut yourself off from us! Confess! Confess!
Prove us right! Do not take our salvation from us!" They held out their
arms to her; implored her; called tenderly to her soul. And suddenly,
across five centuries, we hear that strange murmur, solemn, strong, and
sweet, with its ebb and flow, supplication or threat, a kind of mysterious
chant of unimaginable sadness, superhuman, a chant of death:

"Joan, most dear friend, it is time now, at the end of your trial, to weigh well what has been said. You have already four times been most diligently admonished by the Bishop of Beauvais and the Vicar of the Inquisition, for the honor and reverence due to God, for the peace of men's consciences, the repairing of scandal, and the health of your body; you have heard declared to you the dangers you incur, both to body and soul, if you do not correct and amend yourself and your speech, and submit your acts and words to the Church, accepting her Judgment: nevertheless, until this hour, you have not chosen to obey.

"Now, although several of your Judges might well have found enough to satisfy them in the acts charged against you, yet, in their zeal for the health of your body and soul, these same Judges have ordained that to this end you should be admonished afresh and warned of the errors, scandals, and other misdeeds which you have committed, while at the same time they beg, exhort, and warn you, in the bowels of Our Lord Jesus Christ, Who deigned to suffer so cruel a death for the ransom of mankind, that you should amend your speech, and submit it to the judgment of the Church, as all loyal Christians are bound to do. Do not allow yourself to be separated from Our Lord Jesus Christ, Who created you to share in His Glory: do not choose the path of eternal damnation with the enemies of God, who daily seek to trouble men, by taking on at times the form of Christ, of an angel, or of the Saints, saying and affirming that such indeed they are: as is more fully related in the Lives of the Fathers and in the Scriptures.

"Therefore, if you have been visited by such apparitions, do not choose to believe them; do more, repulse such imaginings and over-credulous fancies; acquiesce in the pronouncements and opinions of the University of Paris and the other Doctors, who well understand the Law of God and the Holy Scriptures. Now, it has seemed to them that no belief must be placed in such apparitions, unless the Holy Scriptures vouchsafe some sufficient sign or miracle. You have had neither one nor the other. You believed these apparitions lightly, instead of turning to God in devout prayer, that He might render you certain; nor had you recourse to any priest or learned ecclesiastic who could give you some assurance. Yet this you should have done, in view of your position and the simplicity of your mind.

"In the first place, Joan, you should consider this: in your King's domains, while you were there, if any knight or other person, born in his king-

dom or owing him obedience, had risen up and said: 'I will not obey the King, or submit to any of his officers,' would you not have said that he ought to be condemned? What then would you say of yourself, you who were born to the faith of Christ, if you do not obey the officers of Christ, that is, the priests of the Church? What judgment will you pronounce on yourself? Refrain, I beseech you, from your utterances, if you love God your Creator, your dearest Spouse and your Salvation; and obey the Church by submitting to her judgments. Know that if you will not do this, if you persist in your error, your soul will be condemned to eternal torment and will suffer forever, while as to your body, I have but little doubt that it will come to perdition.

"Do not allow human respect and a useless shame, which it may be are overmastering you, to hold you back, merely because you have had great honors which, by acting as I suggest, you fear to lose. For we must prefer above all else the honor of God and the well-being of your soul and body; you will lose all if you will not act as I say, for you are separating yourself from the Church and the Faith, to which you made promises in the holy Sacrament of Baptism; you are cutting off the authority of Our Lord from that of His Church, which is nevertheless ruled and governed by His Spirit and Authority. For He said to the priests of His Church: 'He that heareth you, heareth Me, and he that despiseth you, despiseth Me.'

"Diligently considering these matters, in the name of the Bishop of Beauvais and the Vicar of the Inquisition, and of your judges, I admonish, beg, and exhort you, by that devotion you bear to the Passion of your Creator, by that care which you should have for the health of your soul and body, that you correct and amend the above-named errors and return to the way of Truth by obedience to the Church, and by submitting to her judgment and her decisions. By so doing you will save your soul, and (as I hope) preserve your body from death. But if you will not do this, but remain obdurate, then know that your soul will be engulfed in the pit of damnation; while as to the destruction of your body, I greatly fear it. From which may Jesus Christ deliver you!"

The vast murmur of the invisible world slowly died away, then rose again, to sink down once more, and so continued. . . . No human hand now would ever again be able to right the balance which an obscure priest had just disturbed — perhaps unwittingly. The strong sea-swell, which had poured in from the very ends of life at the naming of a sacred Name, carried the little martyr for a moment in the trough of its waves, and then left her stretched out with clenched teeth and closed eyes — already dead. You had once seen her lying thus, old Sire de Gamaches; you had seen her as she lay, fallen to earth from the topmost walls of the redoubt, an arrow through her breast. She had brought ten of her enemies hurtling down with her in the resounding fall, and you, old war-dog, had rushed forward, gripping your axe in both hands. But no one now would come to save her from the pass to which God had brought her. The words she had just heard in silence, humbly, with her dear little head drooping to the earth, had cut her off from all living, from the Holy and Universal Church, from the ransomed world. They had pierced the very center of her soul, the core of her being; they had struck at her pure and tender hope; or rather it was love, her innocent love, it was the dear Name of Jesus which had just broken in her heart. Bishops of Thérouanne and of Noyon, Masters Beaupère, Midi, Erart and Maurice, Graduate Vendères, Graduate Marguerie, she is yours now; take away this prostrate body. She is there, held captive between your hands, and weaker than a little child, with her mad thoughts and her vain honor and all the wrecked dreams of her youth — the Joan who had once boasted of entering by the breach into the good towns she had besieged: *"As to this article, the clerks say that you are a traitress, cunning, cruelly desirous of human bloodshed, seditious."* She, who had held so many others to ransom, was now delivered up in her turn. Dead or alive, she was at last out of danger, in the safe keeping of the men of peace.

If we could learn the secret of that strange moment, we should have the key to all the rest; but the secret is well kept. It seems only as though some thread had snapped which before had bound together all the chief actors of the drama, and for just one moment they were left gesticulating between heaven and earth, like dislocated puppets. From that moment it was herself whom the little martyr had to face, and she did not realize it. Her judges realized it as little as she. Like those insects which lay a worm in the heart of their living prey, they had brought doubt into that childish soul, and now that the loathsome fruit had ripened they no longer recognized their victim. They sought her, they begged her for what, through their fault, she could no longer give them: the pure, untroubled words which would bring them certitude or forgiveness. They had literally stolen her soul. For two more days, with growing impatience, they were to

18

the French Academy, by treating everyone tactfully? God did not make the Church for the prosperity of the saints, but that she might hand down their memory; He made her that the world might not lose, with the divine miracle, a torrent of honor and poetry. What saints have the other churches? *Ours is the Church of the saints.* Whom would you entrust with the charge of this flock of angels? History alone, if left to itself, would have crushed them with its harsh, restricted realism and its summary methods. Our Catholic tradition, without harming them, sweeps them into the full flood of its universal rhythm. They are all there — St. Benedict with his raven, St. Francis with his lute and his Provençal songs, Joan with her sword, Vincent with his shabby soutane — and the newcomer, so strange, so hidden, invoked by contractors and simoniacs, and smiling her incomprehensible smile — Teresa of the Child Jesus. Would one have wished them, during their lifetime, to be kept in glass cases, addressed in rounded periods, knelt to, honored with incense? Such things are all right for Canons. But the saints lived and suffered like us. They bore the full weight of their load, and many of them, without relinquishing it, lay down under it to die. Those of us who dare not yet take to ourselves what was holy and divine in their example, can at least find in it a lesson in heroism and honor. But is there one among us who would not blush to stop short so soon and leave them to follow the endless stretch of road alone? Is there one who could wish to spend his life pondering the problem of evil rather than dashing forward? Who will refuse to liberate the earth? *Our Church is the Church of the saints.* The whole vast machinery of wisdom, strength, supple discipline, glory and majesty, is of itself nothing unless it is animated by love. Yet the lukewarm turn to it only for a guarantee against the risks of the divine. No matter! The smallest little boy in the catechism class knows that the blessing of all the Churchmen put together can only bring peace to those who are ready to receive it — the souls of good will. No rite can dispense us from loving. *Our Church is the Church of the saints.* Nowhere else could one even imagine the adventure — an adventure so human! — of a little heroine who one day passed quietly from the stake of the Inquisition to Paradise, under the noses of a hundred and fifty theologians. *"If we have reached the point"* (wrote Joan's judges to the Pope) *"where sorceresses who prophesy falsely in the name of God, like a certain female taken prisoner within the diocese of Beauvais, are*

better received by the thoughtless populace than are their pastors and doctors,
then all is lost: religion will perish, faith will fail, the Church will be trodden
underfoot, and the iniquity of Satan will prevail throughout the earth!" . . .
And behold, rather less than five centuries later, the image of the sorceress
was exposed for veneration in St. Peter's in Rome — painted, it is true, as
a warrior, and without tabard or divided skirt! — while a hundred feet below her, Joan might have seen, lying prostrated, the tiny figure of a man
in white, who was the Pope himself. Our Church is the Church of the
saints. From the Pope down to the little altar-boy drinking the wine left
over from the cruets, everyone knows that there are not many famous
preachers in the Calendar — not many priest-diplomatists. The only
people to question this are the respectable believers with stomachs and
gold chains, who think that the saints are in far too much of a hurry, and
who would like to go to Heaven with decent deliberation, just as they
walk up to the church-wardens' pew, with the parish priest for company.
Our Church is the Church of the saints. We may respect the Commissariat
Service, the Provost Marshal, the staff officers and the cartographers, but
our hearts are with the men on ahead; our hearts are with those who get
killed. There is not one of us shouldering his burden — his country, his
job, his family — not one of us with our grief-worn faces and our rough-
ened hands, with the unending boredom of our daily life, of daily bread to
be fought for, and the honor of our homes to be defended — there is not
one who will ever have enough theology to become even a Canon. But we
have enough to become saints. We can leave it to others to administer the
Kingdom of God in peace. We have our hands full already, wresting each
hour from the day, one by one, with vast labor — each hour of the inter-
minable day, until that looked-for hour, that unique hour, when God will
deign to breathe upon His exhausted creature. O radiant Death, O true
dawn! Let others look to the spiritual side of things, argue about it, legislate about it; it is the temporal that we hold in both our hands: we hold in
both hands the temporal Kingdom of God. We hold the temporal heritage of the saints. For there were blessed along with us the corn and the
wine, the stone of our thresholds and the roof where the dove builds her
nest; with us were blessed our poor beds full of dreams and forgetfulness;
the highroad down which the country carts go squeaking; the young men
with their pitiless laughter, and the maidens weeping at the fountain's

brink. And ever since then — ever since God Himself has visited us — is there anything in this world which our saints should not have taken back: is there anything at all which they cannot give?

Sermon of an Agnostic
on the Feast of St. Thérèse

TRANSLATED BY PAMELA MORRIS
AND DAVID LOUIS SCHINDLER, JR.

*T*he world shall be judged by children. The spirit of childhood shall judge the world.

Of course the Saint of Lisieux never wrote anything of the kind. Maybe she never had any precise idea of the wondrous spring of which she was the herald. She can hardly have expected, I mean, that one day it would stretch over the earth, and that sweet-smelling tides and snow-white foam would cover towns of steel and reinforced concrete, innocent fields in their terror of mechanical monsters, and even the black-soaked soil of death. "I shall bring forth a shower of roses," she said, twenty years before 1914.

But she didn't know what roses they would be.

*   *   *

You know, sometimes I imagine what any decent agnostic of average intelligence might say, if by some impossible chance one of those intolerable praters were to let him stand awhile in the pulpit, in his stead, on the day consecrated to Saint Thérèse of Lisieux, for instance:

Originally published in Georges Bernanos, *Les Grands cimetières sous la lune* (Paris: Librairie Plon, 1938), pp. 247-75.

23

"Ladies and gentlemen," he would begin, "I don't share your beliefs, but I probably know more about the history of the Church than you do, because I happen to have read it, and not many parishioners can say that. (If I'm wrong, let those who have signify in the usual manner.)

"Ladies and gentlemen, it is well and good to praise the saints as you do, and I am grateful to the priest for allowing me to join in your praising. The saints belong more to you than to me, because you worship the same Master. There's nothing strange about your congratulating yourselves for the glory they've won by their extraordinary lives, but — pardon the observation — I find it hard to believe that they would have endured such struggle and strife only so that you could have such celebrations; celebrations, moreover, that exclude the thousands of poor devils who have never heard of these heroes, and who will never hear of them except for you alone.

"True, every year the Postal Service circulates calendars with the saints' names inscribed alongside the phases of the moon. Indeed, these sublime squanderers have given up everything, even their names, which that other vigilant administration, namely the civil state, has put at the disposal of all comers, believer and unbeliever alike, to serve in the registry for newborn citizens. As for the rest of us, we don't know the saints — and it seems as though you don't know them much more than we do. Who among you is capable of writing twenty lines about his or her patron saint? There was a time when such ignorance puzzled me; now, it seems as normal to me as it does to you.

"Well now, I know you're not inclined to worry much about what people of my sort think. And the most pious among you are even very anxious to avoid all discussion with infidels, in case they were to 'lose their faith,' as they put it. All I can say is their 'faith' must be hanging by a thread. It makes you wonder what the faith of the lukewarm can be! We often call such poor creatures shams and hypocrites; but we can't help feeling rather sad about it all. For though you're not interested in unbelievers, unbelievers are extremely interested in you. There are few of us who at some point in our lives have not made a tentative approach in your direction, were it only to insult you. After all, put yourselves in our place. Were there but one chance, the smallest chance, the faintest chance of your being right, death would come as a devastating surprise to us. So

24

we're bound to watch you closely and try to fathom you. You're supposed to believe in hell. So I think that when you look upon us, your comrades on earth, it might at least be with a fragment of compassion, such as you would not refuse to anyone serving a life-sentence here. Mind you, we're not expecting any ridiculous demonstrations, but still the very thought of your dance-partners, bridge-partners, holiday companions going to grind their teeth and curse their Maker for all eternity — surely that ought to have some effect on you.

"Yes, we were drawn to you. But now we've decided that you're not very interesting after all, and it's rather disappointing. And we hate to think what fools we were, ever to have hoped in you, and to have doubted ourselves, our own unbelief. Most of the people like me rest content with their initial impression. This impression, however, doesn't resolve a thing, for there are clearly among you many insincere Christians who are interesting precisely on account of their instability. But the others remain. Anyone who were to watch them couldn't fail to notice that, though the faith they profess makes little difference in their lives — since they indulge in moderate doses of six of the deadly sins just like everyone else — it poisons their pathetic pleasures by the extreme importance it attaches to the seventh, presumed to be 'mortal.'

"My dear brothers, when you are not possessed of that heroism without which Léon Bloy says a Christian is no more than a pig, it is by the neurotic quality of your lust that you are instantly recognizable. You must *really* believe in hell. You fear it for yourselves. You expect it for us.

"How amazing that in the circumstances you are so entirely lacking in pathos!

"Christian ladies and Christian gentlemen, if ever you were to be filmed unawares, you would be staggered to see on the screen an entirely different person to the motionless double in your mirror. In the same way it is possible that by dint of examination of conscience you have gradually discovered in yourself qualities which with time have grown so familiar to you, that you innocently believe everybody can see them. But we can't see your consciences! On the other hand, your vocabulary is within our reach far more than you are — though for you the meaning has doubtless been weakened by long use. And it makes us wonder! What about that mysterious expression: *in a state of grace*? When you come out of the confes-

25

sional, you're 'in a state of grace.' A state of grace . . . are you sure? Can you blame us if we don't believe it? We're wondering what you do with the Grace of God. Should it not be shining out of you? Where the devil do you hide your joy?

"You'll say that's none of my business. If such joy were given me, I wouldn't know what to do with it. Perhaps. You generally talk in that acid, revengeful way, as though you hated us for the pleasures of which you have deprived yourselves. Can they be so precious in your eyes? Alas, we don't think so much of them. You seem to take us for animals who find in exercising their functions of digestion or reproduction, a source of inexhaustible delight, ever renewed, ever fresh, as though such indulgences were forgotten the instant they were over.

"But I assure you the vanity of vanities has no more secrets for us. The most bitter verses in the Book of Job or Ecclesiastes can teach us nothing we don't already know, and they have already inspired our poets and painters. If you will give the matter thought, I think you will agree that we are rather like the men of the Old Testament. The modern world is as harsh as the Jewish world, and its incessant clamor is the same as that heard by the Prophets, thrown up to the skies from huge cities along the waterside. The silence of death is haunting us also, and we answer it, as they did, by cries of hate and of terror.

"And we worship the same calf. To worship a calf is not, I assure you, the sign of an optimistic people. We are corroded by the same leprosy of which the Semitic imagination bears the hideous wound throughout the centuries: the obsession of nothingness, the impotence — almost physical impotence — to conceive of the Resurrection. Even in the days of Our Lord, with the exception of the small community of Pharisees, the Jewish people had little faith in future life. Perhaps they yearned for it too much — a yearning from the loins, which devours us too. Christian hope never quenches a thirst of that kind, we know. Hope slips through us, as through a sieve. You may say that Israel was awaiting the Messiah. We are awaiting ours. And in the same way again, we are not too sure of his advent: and for fear, also, of seeing our last illusion fly away from us, we rope it firmly to the ground; we dream of a carnal Messiah: Science, Progress, by which we should become masters of the earth.

"Yes, we are men of the Old Testament. You may say that in such

26

case our blindness is even more culpable than theirs. I disagree. In the first place, there is not reason to suppose that we should have crucified the Savior. You cannot get away from the fact that Deicides are of the edifying class. You may say what you like, and try all you can to get away from it, but Deicide can never again be regarded as a crime for the rabble. It is a most distinguished, a very unusual crime reserved for opulent priests, sanctioned by the powerful middle class and the intellectuals. (In those days they were called scribes.)

"You may snicker, my dear brothers, but it isn't the Communists and Blasphemers who crucified Our Lord. And forgive me if I have a good laugh, too. You naturally consider the New Testament inspired, you lay emphasis on each verse of that Holy Book, and can you never have been really struck by the insistence of Jesus on generally white-washing a class of persons, who — to say the least — could hardly have been described as judges, solicitors, retired generals (not forgetting their virtuous spouses) nor even — between ourselves — as the clergy? Aren't you a little disturbed by the fact that God should have reserved His most stringent maledictions for some of the very 'best' people, regular church-goers, never missing a fasting day, and far better instructed in their religion — excepting yourselves of course — than the majority of parishioners today? Doesn't such a huge paradox attract your attention? *We* can't help noticing it, you know.

"It is no answer to say that God has entrusted Himself into your hands. The hands in which Christ entrusted Himself, of yore, were not friendly hands: they were consecrated. That you should have succeeded to the Synagogue, and that such succession should be legitimate, is of no consequence.

"We are waiting to share with you a gift which you proclaim to be priceless, and we don't want to know whether God entrusted Himself to you; we want to know what you are doing with Him!

*   *   *

"My dear brothers and sisters, I can see from here the imperious profile of Colonel Romorantin. He is talking with Mr. Mortgage-holder and several of the clerks familiar to this parish, which is now filled with indignant looks. 'This is *our* parish, after all! This gentleman has never been introduced to us; I do not know him, and he takes advantage of that fact to tell us unpleasant things.' But, my dear Colonel, your Church, after all, is no military society! It would bring me joy to see you take up your throne beneath the vast cupola of the Church Triumphant, but for the time being you are only a candidate like everyone else. Are we celebrating the feast of St. Thérèse or that of the parishioners? To watch you take your place in the choir, I would think I was watching a new member of the Academy being received by his uniformed colleagues. One would think that the sublime doctrine of the Communion of Saints merely adds another prerogative to your already long list. But isn't this doctrine complemented by that of the reversibility of merits? We, the rest of us, answer only for our actions or their material consequences. The solidarity that binds you to others is of a much higher sort. As I see it, the gift of faith that was bestowed upon you, far from granting you freedom, has bound you to them by bonds stronger than flesh and blood.

"You are the salt of the earth. If the world loses its flavor, whom is it I should blame? It is no use to boast of the merits won by your saints, since you are first of all only the stewards of these goods. We often hear the best among you proclaim with pride that they 'owe nothing to anyone.' Coming from your mouths, such words are utterly senseless, for you are literally indebted to everyone, to each of us, to me myself. It is possible, Colonel, that you are riddled with more debts than a junior lieutenant! God alone is privy to our treasuries. If it is true, as your priests say, that the fate of one who holds earthly power may depend, as we speak, on the will of a child torn between good and evil, and who resists grace with all of his feeble strength, nothing is more ludicrous than hearing you speak about the affairs of this world in the most casual tones! Oh, what strange people you are!

"Colonel Romorantin will no doubt say tonight, as he is shuffling the cards, 'What does he mean by that nonsense? My gosh, all of us in this family are implicit believers!' For your morality is ultimately no different from anyone else's: what you call sin is just given a different name by the moralists. Ah, yes! What curious characters you are! When you hear tell that a petite Carmelite with tuberculosis was able, through the heroic practice of duties as humble as she was herself, to obtain the conversion of thousands, or even — why not! — the victory of 1918, you show no sign of contradiction. But if, on the other hand, one were to say to you in all politeness that, according to your own logic, the corruption of the Mexican clergy, for example, is the supernatural cause of the persecutions in this unfortunate country, you shrug your shoulders: 'How could there be any relation between the greed, avarice, or concubinage of those poor priests, and the bloody crimes perpetrated by such monsters here?'

"This reasoning is valid for everyone else in the world, but not for you. This is the reasoning of the judges of this world who punish the adulterer with a five-dollar fine, and lock a beggar away for six months for petty theft. Similarly, you see sense in the claim that the Curé of Ars was able to draw his countryfolk to Mass because of a lifestyle so destitute that his confreres even considered sending the poor man away. But if I had the misfortune of insinuating that Fr. So-and-so from Spain, though perfectly in line with his country's tribunals, might nevertheless be the spiritual father of a parish of murders and sacrilege, I would almost certainly be dealt the Bolshevik treatment. Are all of you imbeciles, or are you just pretending? One might easily overlook the fact that your faith is without works. Because we do not believe in the efficaciousness of your sacraments, we could reproach you for not being better than us only if we were motivated by spite. But what surpasses the understanding is that you habitually reason about the affairs of this world in exactly the same way we do. I mean, who's forcing you? That you act according to our principles, or rather, according to the hard experience of men who, having no hope in another world, fight like animals and plants in this one according to the laws of survival — so be it. But when your fathers profess the pitiless economics of Mr. Adam Smith, or when you give solemn honor to Machiavelli, allow me to say that you cause us no surprise — you simply strike us as odd, incomprehensible fellows.

"This sincere disquisition will not, I know, shake the solid optimism to which you give the name 'hope,' no doubt by analogy. The problem with supernatural virtues is that they have to be practiced with heroism. Things stand with them as they stand with those people who rise to the occasion when provoked, but who are for all of that more easily seduced. Humility dampens the mighty. Cleverly co-opted, the virtue of humility can spare the mediocre the horrors of humiliation, or at least sweeten its bitterness. When circumstances force us to admit that we are not worth the space we occupy, what can we do but close our eyes to such painful evidence? We do not always succeed. To admit to oneself that one is a weakling, a liar, or a scoundrel is hardly comforting to people of our ilk. And yet, when some of you undertake this exercise, you manifest a certain satisfaction that strikes us as somewhat comical. By no grace of God, you read an act of humility in the missalette and come through beaming with self-admiration. Such an operation seems a little too self-serving to be something truly supernatural.

$$* \qquad * \qquad *$$

"Dear friends, I'm afraid my exordium is getting on your nerves. But I was distressed by your bad opinion of us, and I am doing my best to make you revise it. I don't think your opinion is thought out, or deliberate. You see unbelievers as they are, and Christians as they should be — an unfortunate misapprehension. Or rather you see us as indeed we should be, if you were Christians, according to the spirit of the New Testament. For then you would have had the right to condemn our callousness. But do you think it is exactly pleasant to be described daily as the enemies of God by folk so highly supernatural as yourselves? Such a qualification didn't matter very much to our fathers or grandfathers, in the days when your orators were continually invoking against us the sacred rights of freedom of conscience. But for us it might mean the regrettable solicitude of a crusading general.

"No, dear brothers, many unbelievers are not as hardened as you imagine. Need I remind you that God came in Person to the Jewish people. They saw Him. They heard Him. Their hands touched Him. They asked for signs; He gave them those signs. He healed the sick and raised the dead. Then He ascended once again to the Heavens. When we seek Him now, in this world, it is *you* we find, and only you. Oh, I respect the Church — but the history of the Church herself, after all, does not surrender its secret to the first-comer. There is Rome — but you know that the greatness of Catholicism is not immediately apparent, and many of you yourselves come back disappointed. What do you expect from *us*? It is you, Christians, who participate in divinity as your liturgy proclaims; it is you, 'divine men,' who ever since His Ascension have been His representatives on earth.

"Well, you must admit that one would hardly know it at first glance!

*   *   *

"You probably find these observations misplaced, here, within these walls. They are no more misplaced than the presence of most of you. They are certainly quite unworthy of the saint whose feast we celebrate, but they at least have the merit of being simple — even childish. The smile I see from Mr. Mortgage-holder is a sure witness of that fact.

"The Saint whose festival it is this day will not mind my speaking as a child. For I am but a child grown old and burdened with inexperience, and you haven't much to fear from me. Fear those who are to come, who shall judge you. Fear the innocence of children, for they are also *enfants terribles.* Your only way out is to become children yourselves, to rediscover the heart of childhood. For the hour shall strike when questions hurled at you from all points of the earth shall be so urgent and so direct, that you will not be able to answer except by yes or no. The society in which you live seems more complex than others because of its talent for complicating problems, or at least for presenting them under a thousand and one aspects, a talent that allows it to invent by turns provisional solutions which it naturally presents as definitive. Such has been the method in medicine since the time of Molière. But it is likewise now the method followed by economists and sociologists.

"I maintain that you hold an advantageous place in this society, because, by calling itself materialistic, it allows you at small cost the immense privilege of criticizing it in the name of the Spirit. Unfortunately for you, beyond a certain degree of guile and deception, the most insolent of phraseologies cannot mask the void of systems. When a professor hears a particular murmur slowly rising in a hall, barely perceptible as yet, if he piles on authority and gravity, that supreme effort will be his final downfall. You may have read, for example, the following lines that appeared in one of the recent issues of the *Revue de Paris,* authored by a Mr. Paul Morand: 'I can very easily imagine the autarchies of tomorrow prescribing celibacy in certain ill-favored regions, and on the other hand promoting births in more valuable districts, according to some vast embryogenic strategy. After having regulated the quantity of births, the future State will of course focus on the quality — not wanting to remain on this side of the modern State, the director of breeding.' Mr. Paul Morand belongs to the highest society; he is in fact a professional. There are thus no grounds for thinking him a humorist. Since, as far as I can tell, Mr. Patenôtre is no humorist himself, his recent testimonial could be heard by an audience as serious as the one I presently have the honor of addressing:

"'Let us imagine a collectivity as rich as the United States, or even as Great Britain or France, in which we wiped clean any prejudices, *tabula rasa,* and we decided unanimously one fine day to maximize production without regard for the demands of clientele. At once, the factories would perfect their equipment and would run it, day and night, under rotating personnel; likewise, in rural areas, the production of grains, market crops, and livestock would increase their yield.

"'What would be the result? The volume of this agricultural and industrial production, after so many years, would reach such dimensions that we might reasonably imagine a just distribution capable of granting each and every human being a significant comfort-level and a high standard of living.

"'Why, then, must the routine of our methods and the straightjacket of our prejudices oppose the march of progress, halting this high standard of living with the cry, "Thou shall not pass!"? What foul element must thus infect our economic system, imprisoning it in a vicious circle, in which production is restrained by insufficiently solvent consumption, while this rate of consumption is in turn rendered insufficiently solvent, primarily through limited production?'

"I don't know if you appreciate as well as I do the naïveté of this confession. So much energy wasted in creating a self-proclaimed materialistic society that is no longer capable of either producing or selling! You must admit that, in these conditions, the men of order, of a certain order, can dress up in red, in yellow, or in green, dictators can grind their teeth and show the whites of their eyes, and, nevertheless, the kids whose parents have trained them at the theater will begin to exchange glances — having found their Punch and Judy once again! — and the hall will founder in peals of laughter.

"Christians who listen to me — that is your peril! It is difficult to follow upon a society that has foundered in laughter, because even the fragments will be useless. You will have to build it all up again. You will have to build it up under the eyes of children. Become as children yourselves. They have found the chink in your armor, and you will never disarm their irony save by simplicity, honesty, and audacity.

"You will never disarm them save by heroism.

* * *

"In speaking thus, I don't think I am betraying the inspiration of Saint Thérèse of Lisieux. I am simply interpreting it. I am trying to turn it to some human use in the affairs of the world. She preached the spirit of Childhood. The spirit of Childhood is capable of both good and evil. It is not the spirit of resignation to injustice. Nor must you make of it the spirit of revolt, for it would sweep you off the earth.

"This surmise in no way comforts me, for we should be swept too . . .

"For your history, the history of the Church, seems at first only to add a single chapter to History. But this is not at all the case. The prudence and folly of men may be inscribed, one after the other, in the book of history, and still they will never wholly account for the successes and failures. But I know such a thing is not evident at first glance! Moreover, it matters not for example whether one took down, page after page, in basically equivalent proportions, all manner of known errors. I believe that they would not follow upon each other according to any law, that they would not follow the same order of consequence. You explain such singularities through divine assistance. I shall not contradict you on this point. I think, for example, short of being a fool, no one could remain oblivious to the extraordinary quality of your heroes, to their incomparable humanity. Moreover, the name 'hero' is scarcely appropriate for them, and the name 'genius' rings false as well, for the saints are at once heroes and geniuses. But heroism and genius typically occur only at the expense of a certain human quality, while the humanity of your saints abounds. I would thus say that they are at once heroes, geniuses, and children. What great fortune! I don't mind telling you, we would rather deal with them

33

than with you. But, alas!, experience has taught us that all direct contact with them is impossible. What do you think our politicians or moralists would do with a Thérèse of Lisieux? Her message coming from their mouths would lose all meaning, or at least any chance at producing an effect. It was written in your language, and your language alone can express it. We lack the words necessary to translate it without betraying it, and that's all there is to it. My dear brothers and sisters, I make this confession in all humility — please receive it in the same spirit. For if it is you alone who are able to transmit the message of the saints; it is, alas!, necessary that you be the ones responsible for fulfilling this obligation in our regard. I'm sorry to have to tell you that we pay dearly for your neglect.

"And do not try to tell us that these divine human beings came only to add a few finishing touches to the painting. Take, for instance, the message of Saint Francis. This — if you will forgive my presumption — is what he might have said: 'Things are going badly, my children — very badly. And they're going to get a lot worse. I wish I could be more reassuring regarding the state of your health. But if beef-tea was all you required, I'd have stayed quietly at home, for I was very fond of my friends, and I used to accompany myself on the lute, and sing southern songs to them in the evenings. Salvation is within your reach. But it's no good shirking the issue, for there is only one, and it is called Poverty. I am not bringing up the rear, my children, I am preceding you. I am rushing ahead — don't be so frightened. If I were able to suffer alone, you may be sure I wouldn't have interfered with your amusements. But, alas, God does not allow it. You have incensed my Lady Poverty. You have provoked her beyond endurance; because she is so patient, you have subtly, gradually, lifted your entire burden on to her shoulders. Now she lies, always in silence, with her face to the ground, and weeping in the dust. And you think: there's nothing more to get in our way — on with the dance! But you are not going to dance, my children, you are going to die. . . . The malediction of Poverty means death. Follow me!'

"That advice was addressed to all of you. But not many followed it. You are rather like the legendary Italian soldiers waiting to attack. All of a sudden the colonel snatches up his saber, jumps over the parapet, and charges off beneath heavy fire, all by himself, crying *Avanti! Avanti!* Whilst his soldiers remain crouching under cover, electrified by such a display of valor, clapping loudly, with tears in their eyes: *Bravo! Bravo! Bravissimo!*

"My dear brothers, I keep on saying the same thing, because it always is the same thing. Had you followed that saint instead of applauding, Europe would never have known the Reformation, nor the religious wars, nor this horrible Spanish Crusade. Saint Francis was calling to you, but death did not pick and choose: death descended on us all. The danger is the same today. It must be even greater. The Saint of Lisieux, whose prodigious career is sufficient token in itself of the tragic urgency of the message entrusted to her, asks you to become as children. The purpose of God is impenetrable, as you say. Yet I cannot help feeling that this is your last chance. Your last chance — and ours. Are you capable of rejuvenating our world or not?

"The New Testament is eternally young, it is you who are so old. And your 'old men' are even older than the oldest of you. They go wagging their heads and mumbling: 'We don't want either Fascists or Communists,' in voices so hollow and cracked that they spew out a tooth at every syllable. Reaction is essential, and we could do with a revolution! But not all your reactions and revolutions put together would suffice. God, can't you forget your decrepit scruple of preserving an order which no longer spares itself, which is destroying itself? Besides, universal order has been replaced by general mobilization. Call back your casuists, before they get mobilized too! Call 'em back, or rather — take 'em away. For the poor things have been indulging in such involved contortions that their legs are round their necks, and their arms are dug into their shoulders, and their heads are on a level with their lowest vertebrae. Carry them home just as they are, on your stretchers, for they'll never get unknotted by themselves.

"Nothing has been really lost in these two thousand years of useless negotiations, for the New Testament has reached us intact, not a comma missing. Is it therefore so hard merely to answer yes or no to all future questions? Men of honor talk thus. Honor belongs also to childhood. Because it is based on childhood, it is able to escape the analysis of moralists, for your moralist only torments the 'mature' fabulous creatures which he has invented for the convenience of his own deductions. There are no mature men, there is no intermediary state between one age and the next.

35

Whoever cannot give more than he receives will surely fall to dust. What morality or physiology has to say regarding such a factor of great importance is of no consequence to us, because we give to the words of youth and age an entirely different meaning. The knowledge of men — and not the experience of men — soon teaches us that youth and age are a matter of character, or soul, if you prefer. A kind of predestination. You will agree that these views are no innovation. The most obtuse observer knows perfectly well that a miser is old at twenty.

"There is a country of the Young. That country is calling to you, that country must be saved. Do not wait for the country of the Old to finish destroying it by those same methods which, in less than a century, not so long ago, defeated the Redskins. You must not let the Young be colonized by the Old! Don't imagine that your words are sufficient protection — even when they get printed. In the days when the American Pharisees were methodically exterminating a race a thousand times more precious than their own foul conglomeration, did not the sham Indians of Chateaubriand and Cooper share with the sham Scots of Walter Scott, the cozy leisure of romantically-minded old maids, wallowing in pity, as in freshly-spilt blood? The advent of Joan of Arc in the twentieth century has the character of a solemn warning. The remarkable fate of an obscure little Carmelite girl seems to me an even more serious sign.

"Christians, hurry up and become children again, that we may become children too. It can't be so very difficult. Because you do not live your faith, your faith has ceased to be a living thing. It has become abstract — bodiless. Perhaps we shall find that the disincarnation of the Word of God is the real cause of all our misfortune. Many of you use the truths of the New Testament as initial themes out of which you compose a kind of orchestral variation inspired by worldly wisdom. In your endeavor to justify these truths in the eyes of political doctrinaires, are you not afraid of placing them beyond the reach of simple men? Why not — just for once — oppose them, just as they are, to our complicated systems, and then wait, quietly wait for the answer, without talking all the time?

"Joan of Arc was but a girl-saint, yet she put the Paris Doctors of Divinity in a tight spot. Why not let the Christ-Child have His say? You may suggest that's none of my business. I beg your pardon: to get the better of an order almost as petrified as yours, so many Doctors were unnecessary!

That is a historical fact of great significance. I quite understand that you should be attached to your libraries. They have been of great use against arch-heretics. But the world is not merely being poisoned by arch-heretics, it is obsessed by the idea of suicide. From one end of the planet to the other, it is hurriedly piling up all the necessary adjuncts to this gigantic enterprise. You won't snatch a man from suicide by proving to him that suicide is anti-social, because the poor devil is planning to desert, by means of death, a society which disgusts him. And you go on urging men, in a manner barely distinct from the Moralists — the Morality-Machines — to check their desires! But they have no desires! They have no longer any purposes. They can discover none that is worth an effort.

"Christian ladies and Christian gentlemen, I am coming to the end of my long harangue. As an agnostic, I regret being unable to give you my blessing. I remain your very humble servant. To feel much as you do, almost as disconcerted as yourselves in face of these formidable times, is just a little heart-rending. Because, forgive my frankness if I say that you are just as anxious to save your skins as we are. The slogan of crazy despair — never mind what happens so long as I get out! — is about to be shaped on your lips, whilst your eyes steal glances at Dictatorships. Anybody, anyhow! What the hell! Get back to childhood, it's not as dangerous.

"We're bound to say that we haven't the slightest confidence in your political capacity. Soon your excess of zeal will have compromised you, even with your new masters. To become the pet aversion of free men, and of the poor, with a program like the New Testament, is rather ludicrous, don't you agree? Become as little children — there lies your refuge. And when the Powerful of the world ask you insidious questions about all kinds of dangerous problems, such as 'modern warfare,' 'the respect of treaties,' 'capitalistic organization,' don't be ashamed to confess that you're too foolish to make any reply, and that the Lord Jesus shall answer for you.

"For then the Word of God may perhaps work the miracle of rallying together men of good will, since it is for them that it was spoken. *Pax hominibus bonae voluntatis* could hardly be translated into: 'First we'll have a war, and we'll see later,' could it?

"I know it is a paradox for us to be awaiting a miracle. But it would be an even greater paradox to await it from you. Therefore we take precautions. We feel we have every right because, mind you, we do not claim to interpret the New Testament, we call upon you to carry it out, according to your belief, and the belief of your Church. We do not refute your learned doctors. We refute your political meddlers, because they have given us abundant proof of their presumption and stupidity. The Gospel! The Gospel! When finally you stake everything on a miracle, it is only natural to insist that the experiment should be faultlessly carried out.

"Supposing, my brothers, that I were consumptive, and I wished to drink the waters of Lourdes, and doctors suggested that they should dilute in it some drug of their own. 'My dear doctors,' I would reply, 'you have said I was incurable. Let me try my luck undisturbed. In this matter, which is strictly between myself and Our Lady, if I need any go-between, you can be sure I won't be asking the pharmacist.'"

Dialogues of the Carmelites

TRANSLATED BY MICHAEL LEGAT

PUBLISHER'S NOTE

Dialogues des Carmélites was written by Georges Bernanos in Tunisia during the winter 1947-48. The work was destined for a film, and the author of *Joy* found in this subject — in the story of Blanche de la Force, dominated by fear, but finally accepting her martyrdom — perhaps the main preoccupation of his spiritual life and work.

Bernanos's scenario was based on an earlier film version written by Father Raymond Bruckberger, in turn adapted from the *novelle* by Gertrud von le Fort, *The Song from the Scaffold*. Bernanos, who had read this novel previously, did not refer to it while working on the Bruckberger scenario, which he rewrote almost entirely. Here he abridged a scene, here he gave another more weight or modified its meaning, rewriting the descriptions of scenery or grouping, and omitting anything which weakened the spiritual force of the narrative. So was born a work which properly belongs to him.

The diary in which from January to March 1948 he scrupulously recorded the employment of his time, until the day when illness finally interrupted it, is tremendous in its impact. Already ill, he devoted working days of eight and ten hours to his *Dialogues,* of which the successive MSS show the mark. And the thoughts which he noted there concerning his *Life of Jesus,* which he had been contemplating for fifteen years, prove to what extent, feeling himself gravely afflicted, he lived in contemplation of death, preparing himself for it as for an Imitation of the Holy Agony.

Dialogues des Carmélites was completed by mid-March, when Bernanos took to the bed from which he was not to arise. Faithful to the method of work which he had always followed, he had made a fair copy of the text transcribing in his fine, clear hand the prose he had finally distilled from the innumerable corrections in the almost illegible notebooks in which his first draft was written. Towards the end, however, the second MS shows a more hasty writing, with fairly numerous alterations, which called for careful interpretation. The definitive version, which filled ten small exercise books, was copied by Mme. Arnel Guerne, Bernanos's voluntary secretary at that time. It is that copy which, following careful comparison with the MSS, served as the basis for the French edition published by Les Editions du Seuil.

The French publishers added only that which, omitted from the text destined for filming, they considered necessary for the comprehensibility of a reading version; that is to say, the résumé of the scenes which, having no dialogue, were not rewritten by Bernanos. These scenes were drafted with reference to both the scenario and to Gertrud von Le Fort's *novelle*. The reader will be able to recognize these passages without difficulty, as all that does not appear in the MSS is printed in italics, viz. Scenes I and II of the Prologue, Scene II of Part Two, Scenes IV and V of Part Three, Scenes IV and V of Part Four, and Scenes I, IV, XIII, and XVII of Part Five. It has been felt unnecessary to distinguish typographically the few scenes which have been borrowed literally from the scenario, Bernanos having made them his own by copying them into his MS or by leaving space for them to appear.

The division into five parts does not appear in the MS, which follows the continuity of the scenario. It seemed to facilitate the reading, without affecting the work as conceived by Bernanos.

Finally, in the scenes where the Community is assembled together, certain lines have been attributed to one or other of the Sisters, as Bernanos did not always indicate the allocation of these lines, no doubt intending to do so before the book finally went to press.

THE ENGLISH-SPEAKING READER who is anxious to know exactly how much of the conception of the characters and the spiritual meaning given to the dialogue is Bernanos's own should refer to Gertrud von Le

Fort's *novelle, The Song from the Scaffold,* an English translation of which is published in America by Sheed and Ward Inc. It would be interesting, too — but space does not permit a detailed investigation here — to know exactly how much of the German novel and the French scenario is historical fact. We must limit ourselves to the intimation, with the support of certain facts,[1] that Gertrud von Le Fort — though finding her inspiration in the true story of the sixteen Carmelites of Compiègne who were guillotined on July 17th, 1794, in Paris — made full use of the Romantic freedom of the imagination. Marie-Françoise de Croissy, Mère Henriette de Jesus, born in 1745, was indeed Prioress of the Carmel, but from 1779 to 1785, when she was succeeded by Madeleine Lidoine, Mère Thérèse de Saint-Augustin, born in 1752. As for Mother Marie of the Incarnation, she not only existed but survived her Sisters and became their first historian. Born in 1761 in Paris, her name was Françoise-Geneviève Philippe, but everything leads to the belief that she was the illegitimate child of a person of noble if not of royal blood. Miraculously healed of paralysis, she entered Carmel in 1786, and was in Paris on personal business when her Sisters were arrested. She went into hiding, and all trace of her is lost until 1823, when she went to live at the Carmel of Sens as a pensioner, and where she died in 1836. It was there that she wrote the *Relation,* which serves as common source for all works on the Carmelites of Compiègne. This very remarkable account gives the most vivid portraits of the majority of the Sisters.

The other victims of the execution on July 17th, 1794, were: Marie-Anne Brideau, Sœur Saint-Louis, sub-Prioress, born at Belfort in 1752; Anne-Marie Thouet, Sœur Charlotte de la Résurrection, born in Mouy (Oise) in 1715; Marie-Anne Piedcourt, Sœur de Jesus Crucifié, born in Paris in 1715; Catherine-Charlotte Brard, Sœur Euphrasie de l'Immaculée-Conception, born in Bourth (Eure) in 1736; Marie-Antoinette Hanisset, Sœur Thérèse du Coeur de Marie, born in Rheims in 1742; Marie-Gabrielle Trézel, Sœur Thérèse de Saint-Ignace, born in Compiègne in 1743; Rose Chrétien de la Neuville, Sœur Julie, born in Loreau (Eure-et-Loir) in 1741; Anne Pebras, Sœur Marie-Henriette de la Providence, born in Cajarc (Lot) in 1760; Antoinette Roussel, Sœur du Saint-Esprit,

---

1. Cf. the account by Victor Pierre, *Les Seize Carmélites de Compiègne* (Lecoffre, 1905), which Bernanos may have consulted.

born in Fresnes in 1742: Marie Dufour, Sœur Sainte-Marthe, born in Beaune in 1742; Juliette Verolot, Sœur Saint-Françoise, born in Laighes in 1764; the two Turn-Sisters,[2] Catherine and Thérèse Soiron, born in Compiègne in 1742 and 1751; finally, the youngest, Marie-Jeanne Meunier, Sœur Constance, born in Saint-Denis in 1766.

The last-mentioned Sister deserves special attention. For if Blanche de la Force does not figure in this list of the sixteen martyrs, Gertrud von Le Fort did not entirely invent the central character whose dramatic story she imagined. From Marie-Jeanne Meunier she constructed the two young novices, Constance de Saint-Denis and Blanche of the Agony of Christ. It is known, in fact, that Sister Constance entered Carmel on May 29th, 1788, where her Clothing took place the following December 30th, and was about to make her Profession when a decree dated December 1789 prevented her.[3] Her brother then came to reclaim her, but the young novice refused to return to her family.[4] Neither did she yield to the pressure of the Commissaries. There the resemblance ends.

The inventory of the convent took place on August 4th, 1790, the interrogation of the Sisters on the next day, and their expulsion on September 14th, 1792. They lived thereafter, dispersed in small groups, in the town of Compiègne, until their arrest on June 22nd, 1794, their transfer to La Conciergerie[5] a few days later, and the condemnation of July 17th, the sentence being carried out forthwith. Constance Meunier was the first to die; they all mounted the scaffold singing the *Salve Regina,* followed by the *Veni Creator.*

2. The Turn-Sisters are not religious, but servants, in charge of the turn, a type of revolving cupboard used in Enclosed Orders, by means of which goods may be passed into or out of the convent, thus avoiding direct contact with the outside world. Sometimes known as a "wheel." *Translator.*

3. The Clothing marked the end of the Sister's service as a postulant, and she then became a novice. After a further year, she made her Profession, and soon afterwards received the black veil. She remained a novice for three years longer, but no ceremony marked the end of her novitiate. This procedure was modified with the promulgation of the New Code of Canon Law. *Translator.*

4. This circumstance, which Gertrud von Le Fort did not utilize, plays an important part in Bernanos's work.

5. A prison within the Palais de Justice in Paris, in which during the Revolution condemned prisoners were held pending execution. *Translator.*

TRANSLATOR'S NOTE

I wish to acknowledge with much gratitude the kindness of friends who have advised me on procedure in Carmel. Their comments have been invaluable; among them I feel I must mention the following inaccuracies which exist in Bernanos's original text:

Part Two, Scene IX. The vigil. The directions indicate that Blanche and Constance are kneeling on prie-dieux. In actual fact, Carmelite Sisters kneel unsupported.

Part Three, Scene IV. The Ceremony of Blanche's taking of the veil. Bernanos uses the expression *prise de voile,* but this phrase is more usually associated with the making of the Profession. The ceremony he is referring to is generally known as the Clothing.

Part Four, Scene XII. The vow of Martyrdom. Vows in Carmel are made into the hands of the Prioress, or quite privately, but never into the hands of a presiding priest. Furthermore, novices would be the last, not the first, to pronounce. A version of this scene based on historical fact would have shown the Prioress reading in the name of the Community an act of consecration (not a vow), to which the Sisters then assented.

Finally, it should be emphasized that *The Fearless Heart* is an imaginative work, and that no historically accurate portrayal is intended of those persons who in fact existed and whose real names have been used (the two Prioresses, Mother Marie, Sister Constance, and Sister Marthe). Equally, many of the events of the narrative are imaginary, either wholly or in part.

M.R.L.

List of Characters

The Marquis de la Force
The Marquise de la Force
The Chevalier, *their son*
Blanche, *their daughter* (Sister Blanche of the Agony of Christ)
Mme de Croissy (Mother Henriette of Jesus), *Prioress of the Carmel at
   Compiègne*
Mme Lidoine (Mother Marie of St. Augustine), *the new Prioress*
Mother Marie of the Incarnation, *sub-Prioress*
Mother Jeanne of the Child Jesus, *the oldest Sister*
Mother Gérald ⎱ *older nuns*
Sister Claire ⎰
Sister Antoine, *in charge of the turn*
Sister Catherine
Sister Félicité
Sister Gertrude
Sister Alice
Sister Valentine of the Cross
Sister Mathilde
Sister Anne
Sister Marthe
Sister St. Charles ⎱ *very young Sisters*
Sister Constance de St. Denis ⎰
The Chaplain of the Carmel

M. Javelinot, *the doctor*
The Marquis de Guiches
Gontran
Héloise
Rose Ducor, *actress*
The convent notary
Thierry, *a lackey*
Antoine, *the coachman*
Delegates from the municipality, commissaries, officials
Prisoners, guards, commoners

"In one way fear is also God's daughter, redeemed on the night of Holy Friday. She is not beautiful to look at — oh no! — ridiculed at times, at others cursed, disowned by everyone . . . and yet, make no mistake about it, she is present at every deathbed — she is man's intercessor."

La Joie (Joy)

Prologue

Scene I

1774. The Place Louis XV in Paris, on the evening of the festivities held to celebrate the marriage of the Dauphin, the future Louis XVI, to the Archduchess Marie Antoinette. The carriages of the aristocrats pass through the midst of the happy crowd, which is controlled by the military. In one carriage a young couple can be seen: the Marquis de la Force and his wife, who is pregnant. The Marquis alights from the coach and moves off towards the stands.

The fireworks display begins, but suddenly some boxes of rockets take fire and explosions follow. Although there is no serious danger, the crowd is seized with panic. Turmoil; frightened cries; some fall to the ground and are trampled on. The young Marquise bolts the carriage door. The coachman whips the horses, and they shy and set off at a mad gallop. The crowd suddenly becomes angry; they stop the horses, and a window-pane is smashed in splinters. A man shouts: "Things will be different soon — it'll be you people who are massacred, and we shall be riding in your carriages!" The soldiers arrive in time to free the Marquise, whom the crowd was about to ill-treat.

Scene II

A few hours later. A doctor comes from the Marquise's bedroom in the Hôtel de la Force. He announces to the Marquis that a daughter has just been born to him, but that the young mother is dead.

Part One

Scene I

The Hôtel de la Force. April 1789. The Marquis and the Chevalier are present. The latter is obviously surprised by his father's presence, but he cannot restrain the question which is burning on his lips.

THE CHEVALIER. Where is Blanche?

THE MARQUIS. Damme, I know not. Why the devil do you not ask her women instead of bursting in on me without warning, like an ill-mannered boor?

THE CHEVALIER. I humbly beg your pardon.

THE MARQUIS. At your age there is no great harm in being a little bois-terous, just as it is natural, at my age, to be a creature of habits. Your uncle's visit has made me forgo my afternoon nap and, to tell the truth, I was feeling a little sleepy just now. But why do you want Blanche?

THE CHEVALIER. Roger de Damas, who has just left here, has had to turn back twice to avoid being caught up in a great mob of people. The rumor is that they are going to burn Reveillon's effigy in the Place de Grève.

THE MARQUIS. Well, let them burn it! With wine to be had for two sous, one must expect the spring to make their heads spin. It will all pass.

THE CHEVALIER. If I dared in your presence to play the sorry wit, I should reply that in so far as my sister's carriage is concerned, you are

51

unlikely to prove a very reliable prophet. It cannot pass; Damas saw her stopped by the crowd at the Carrefour de Bucy.

The Marquis, who had opened his snuff-box, snaps the lid to without taking any snuff from it, and as the Chevalier comes nearer him, pushes him gently away with his outstretched hand.

THE MARQUIS. The carriage . . . the crowd . . . forgive me, but those spectres have haunted my dreams too often in the past. . . . Nowadays they speak freely enough of riots and even of revolution, but those who have not seen a mob stricken by panic have seen nothing. . . . 'Sdeath, those faces with the snarling mouths, the thousand upon thousand eyes. . . . Merciful heavens! In a single moment the whole square began to seethe from one end to the other, and you could see hats and sticks flying up above them to a prodigious height, as if shot into the air by the explosion of a deafening shout. Some who were there have sworn to me since that they did not see the hats and the sticks, but I saw them, by all the devils of Hell!

THE CHEVALIER. Forgive me, sir — I should have known better. . . . I have spoken like a fool once more.

The Marquis has taken up his snuff-box again. He taps the lid with his fingertips, his thoughts far away.

THE MARQUIS. Bah! Now even my old head starts spinning in a trice. But what is there in common, I ask you, between what I witnessed then and some seasonal little riot or other, some procession of drunkards through the streets of Paris? My carriage is solidly built, the old horses are not easily affrighted, Antoine has been in our service for twenty years, and the two footmen used to be soldiers in the Navarre Regiment. Nothing untoward can happen to your sister.

THE CHEVALIER. Oh, I have no fear for her safety, you know that — but for her unhealthy imagination.

THE MARQUIS. Blanche is, indeed, too sensitive by far. A good marriage will put that to rights. Come, come! A pretty girl has the right to be a little afraid. Be patient! She will present you with nephews who will be the finest devil-may-care young rips you may wish for.

THE CHEVALIER. Believe me, it cannot be fear alone that endangers Blanche's health, perhaps her life. Or rather, it is suppressed fear, in the depths of her being, the frost in the heart of the bud. . . . Yes, believe me, sir, my sister's humor holds something beyond ordinary comprehension. And perhaps in a less enlightened century than our own . . .

THE MARQUIS. What's that! You are talking like some superstitious country bumpkin, sir. The affection in which you have always held your sister is warping your judgment. More often than not Blanche appears to me quite normal — sometimes even sprightly.

THE CHEVALIER. Oh, no doubt. She sometimes deludes even me, and I should believe the spell broken could I not always read its curse in her eyes. Yes, her look reveals what her voice may hide; it is in the eyes, not in the voice, that fear betrays itself. That it has been my lot to learn in the King's service, though I am still a novice in it. . . . But I have no need to tell you what more serious wars had already taught you long before I was born.

The Marquis begins a gesture of denial, then replies slowly with the air of a man who is searching among his memories.

THE MARQUIS. In faith, that is true, we knew those things and they were sometimes useful to us. But they come strangely to me from your lips, for we did not reason things out — such is the difference between our generation and yours. Why the devil should I think of judging your sister from my experience of corporals and sergeants of the Royal-Picardy? Beware of reasoning everything out as you are doing today — you risk no longer being able to understand the reason for anything! When Blanche and her governess are here — very soon — you will laugh at your distress, and she at hers.

THE CHEVALIER. You mean that once more she will have escaped with no more than a fright. . . . Escaped with a fright! In speaking of Blanche, the relation of those two words one to the other makes me tremble. . . . So noble, so proud a creature! Yet the canker is within her as the maggot is within the fruit. . . . Oh, sir, such language must seem to you obscure and high-flown, the more so from my lips. . . . Sift from it, I pray you, only that which will decide you to send my sister to

Miromesnil, or perhaps to Limeuil, where she may take the spring air and drink the fresh milk from our herds.

THE MARQUIS. Yes, and play at being a farmer's wife, as is the fashion to-day. Unfortunately that is no way for a young woman to secure an establishment. I should be a fool indeed to send my daughter away just as I begin to congratulate myself, with good cause, on the attentions of your friend. Oh, young Damas may not pass for what used to be called a good match, but I would willingly make him my son-in-law. Why not? I sometimes think the young people of today are a little too complex for my taste. But he is a real Frenchman, a Frenchman, one might say, belonging to three centuries: he has the chivalry of one, the grace of another, and the gaiety of our own. Yes, indeed, I would say he is a good Frenchman, a handsome lad, a brave lad, a man of taste, and a nobleman of the French court — that is Roger de Damas for you. But, gracious heavens, you think of him as I do.

THE CHEVALIER. He is my best friend, that says it all. . . . But do not deceive yourself. While she is in this wretched condition, my sister will never marry a man who is known everywhere as more foolhardy than most, and before whom she would fear perhaps to blush.

THE MARQUIS. Childishness!

THE CHEVALIER. Do not be oversure. I do not know whether the strangeness of her disposition will lead Blanche into some shameful action, shameful at least according to the ideas she holds of the duties of a nobleman's daughter, but I am convinced that she would not survive such disgrace.

The door opens and Blanche appears on the threshold, unobtrusively enough for the spectator to wonder whether she heard the last few words or not. The Chevalier cannot restrain a gesture, but the old Marquis has better control over his nerves, and says in a very natural tone:

THE MARQUIS. Blanche, your brother was exceeding anxious to see you again.

Blanche's face shows signs of great distress, but she has evidently had time to collect herself, and she makes an effort to speak brightly.

BLANCHE. M. le Chevalier is too kind to his little hare. . . .

THE CHEVALIER. Why do you repeat at every turn a jest which has no meaning except for the two of us?

BLANCHE. Hares are not in the habit of spending the daytime away from their forms. It is true that I take my lair with me. But a mere pane of glass between that crowd and my trembling person seemed to me for a moment, I assure you, a quite contemptible protection. I must have looked ludicrous indeed.

The Marquis signs to his son to keep silent.

THE MARQUIS. Damme! We will talk of your adventures at supper, when you have rested a little. Better to forget for the time what you have seen — and you must not judge that rabble by their faces. . . . The people of Paris are kindhearted devils, and always end their uproars by singing.

THE CHEVALIER. M. de Damas, who saw you at the Bucy crossroads, has just told me that through the carriage windows you looked quite composed. . . .

She blushes with pleasure, and in order to hide her anxiety she speaks with an increasing vivacity, which eventually creates an atmosphere of vague unease. The Marquis and his son exchange a glance.

BLANCHE. Oh, M. de Damas no doubt saw only that which he wished to see. . . . But did I really look quite composed? In faith, perhaps danger is akin to cold water — it takes your breath away at first, but is not as disagreeable when you have plunged in up to your neck. And besides, what chance are we girls given to prove our mettle? To show our worth we must first know what our worth is. . . . As I live, when I alighted from the carriage just now Mme Janin could not believe her eyes, I was so light-hearted. . . . This weight that I have always borne on my heart. . . . *(She places her hand on her breast, looks around her, and stops short)* But what am I saying? I am a foolish creature, forgive me. . . . *(Before her brother can open his mouth, she continues in tones whose gaiety is no longer more than assumed)* The ceremony at the

Dames de la Visitation was very long and tired me prodigiously. No doubt, that is why I am talking nonsense. With your permission, Father, I will follow your advice and take a little rest before supper. Look! How fast the daylight is fading this evening. . . .

THE MARQUIS. I should believe a storm to be threatening were it not so early in the season. The sky suddenly became overcast while you were speaking.

She moves towards the staircase, her brother accompanying her.

THE CHEVALIER. As you are retiring to your room, order candles to be brought at once and do not stay there without companions. I know the twilight always makes you melancholy. You used to tell me when you were small: "Each night I die, so as to return from the dead each morning."

BLANCHE. There has only been one morning ever, M. le Chevalier — Easter morning. But each night entered upon is the night of the Holy Agony.

She goes out.

THE MARQUIS. Her imagination always jumps from one extreme to another. What the devil is the meaning of that last remark?

THE CHEVALIER. I do not know. What does it matter? 'Tis her look and her voice that go to your heart. The horses will be unharnessed by now. I shall go and question old Antoine.

He goes out. As the door closes a cry of terror is heard. For a moment the Marquis hesitates which direction to take, then moves towards the staircase. Footsteps are heard on the stairs. The Marquis appears to recognize someone in the half-light, and calls:

THE MARQUIS. Is that you, Thierry?

The footsteps approach and a young footman appears. He is very pale.

THE MARQUIS. What is it, lad?

56

THE FOOTMAN. I was lighting the candles when Mlle Blanche came into the room. . . . I think she saw first of all my shadow on the wall. I had pulled the curtains.

Scene II

Blanche's room. As her father enters, Blanche goes up to him. Her voice, her attitude, her features display a kind of resolution and desperate resignation.

THE MARQUIS. In coming up to you, instead of calling your governess, I gave way to my first impulse. Forgive my impoliteness. I see that by good fortune there is nothing grievously amiss.

BLANCHE. Oh, sir, you are the most indulgent and courteous of parents.

THE MARQUIS. M. Rousseau, who was not the best of examples, desires us to be the friends of our children. When all is said and done, I fear that friendship may one day cause us regret for our indulgence and courtesy, for really it is we whom it favors. It is easier to be a friend than a parent. . . . But let us speak no more of this little incident.

BLANCHE. There is no incident so negligible, Papa, that the Will of God is not inscribed upon it, as all Heaven is seen in a drop of water. Yes, it is God who brings you here to listen to that which so often I have lacked the courage to tell you. I have decided to enter Carmel.

THE MARQUIS. Carmel!

BLANCHE. I think such a confession surprises you less than you wish it to appear to do.

THE MARQUIS. Alas! There is always cause to fear the urgings of a fanatic devotion in a young person as virtuous as my daughter. It is true that certain unhappy circumstances surrounding your birth have bound me most tenderly to you, and I would not restrain you in any way. So we will talk more of this in due time, but remember henceforth that you are doubtless overestimating not your courage but your strength and your health. . . .

BLANCHE. My courage . . .

THE MARQUIS. A girl with less pride would not torment herself over a mere cry of fright.

BLANCHE. My courage . . .

She speaks with sudden decision, as if in forcing herself to convince her father she were gradually giving way to the hope of convincing herself.

BLANCHE. In faith, yes, I believe indeed that there is more than one element in my character for which you would not have to blush. In making me as I am, why should God have wished only to humiliate me? The weakness of my nature is not merely a humiliation which He imposes on me, but the sign of His Will in His poor handmaid. Far from feeling the shame of it, I should rather be tempted to find glory in such a destiny. Oh, doubtless it is quite improper, even in your presence, to quote to my advantage the blood from which I spring, the lustre of our family. No matter! By what miracle could I have been born entirely unworthy of so many fine men, justifiably renowned for their valor? There are several kinds of courage. One is certainly to face musket-fire bravely. Another is to sacrifice the advantages of an enviable position to go and live among companions and under the authority of superiors whose birth and education are often quite inferior to one's own.

She stops, a little embarrassed. The old Marquis listens in silence, his head low. Then, with an effort, he speaks, but in the tones of a man who in speaking performs a duty:

THE MARQUIS. My daughter, there is in your resolution more pride than you think. I certainly could not be considered a devout man, but I have always believed that people of our rank should act honestly towards God. One does not renounce the world out of resentment, like a recruit who, for fear of being a coward, lets himself be killed in his first warm engagement, uselessly depriving his King and Country of his services.

She reels visibly under this imputation, but she does not yield.

BLANCHE. I do not scorn the world; it is scarcely true to say I fear it.

The world is simply for me an element in which I cannot live. No, Father, I cannot physically support its noise, its restlessness; the best of company dispirits me; the very bustle of the streets stuns me; and if I wake in the night, despite myself I hear through the thickness of our curtains and the bed-hangings the sound of this great indefatigable city which only sleeps at dawn. Relieve me of this burden on my nerves and we shall see what I am capable of. What! would you reproach a young officer for resigning from service in the King's ships if he could not support the sea?

THE MARQUIS. My dearest child, it is for your conscience alone to decide whether the burden is beyond your strength to bear or not.

BLANCHE. Oh, Father, let us stop this play of cat and mouse, for pity's sake! For pity's sake, let me believe that there is a cure for this wretched weakness which is ruining my life. Alas! M. de Damas must be blind indeed where I am concerned to have thought me quite composed just now. God! I could scarce sit upright amidst the cushions. I was frozen to the marrow — I am still — feel my hands. . . . Oh, Father, Father! If I did not hope that Heaven has some purpose for me, I should die of shame here at your feet. It is possible that you are right and the burden has not yet fully descended upon me — but God will not hold that against me. I sacrifice everything to Him, abandon everything, renounce everything, so that He may restore my integrity.

Part Two

Scene I

A few weeks later.

The parlor of the Carmel at Compiègne. The Prioress and Blanche are talking on either side of the double grille which is covered by a black veil. Mme de Croissy, the Prioress, is an old woman, visibly ill. She tries awkwardly to move her armchair nearer the grille. With difficulty she manages to do so, and, smiling, speaks a little breathlessly:

THE PRIORESS. Do not imagine that this armchair is a privilege of my rank, like the stool on which a duchess may sit in the presence of the King. Alas! Out of charity for my dear daughters who concern themselves so eagerly for my comfort, I should like to feel at my ease in it. But it is difficult to renew old habits, forgotten so long ago, and I can see clearly that something which should be an alleviation will never be more for me than a humiliating necessity.

BLANCHE. It must be good, Reverend Mother, to know oneself so far advanced along the road of renunciation that it is no longer possible to turn back.

THE PRIORESS. My poor child, habit ends by renouncing all else. But of what worth is it that a religious should have renounced everything if she has not renounced herself, that is to say, renounced her own renunciation? *(A silence)* I see that the severities of our Rule do not alarm you.

BLANCHE. They draw me on.

THE PRIORESS. Yes, yes, you have a generous spirit. *(Silence)* But remember that those obligations which appear the lightest are quite often, in practice, the most oppressive. One may swallow a camel and strain at a gnat.

BLANCHE. *(Swiftly)* Oh, Reverend Mother, there is more to fear than these little sacrifices. . . . *(She stops in embarrassment)*

THE PRIORESS. Oh yes? And what are these fine causes of fear?

BLANCHE. *(Speaking with less and less assurance)* Reverend Mother, I could not . . . it would be difficult for me . . . thus . . . just now. . . . But with your permission I shall ponder on it and will reply to you later.

THE PRIORESS. As you wish. . . . Would you answer me straightway if I asked you what is your conception of a Carmelite's first obligation?

BLANCHE. To conquer one's nature.

THE PRIORESS. Very good. To conquer and not coerce — the difference is of some consequence. By forcing one's nature one merely succeeds in becoming artificial, and what God asks of His daughters is not that they should play-act each day for His benefit, but that they should serve Him. A good servant is always in her rightful place and never calls attention to herself.

BLANCHE. I only ask to pass unnoticed. . . .

THE PRIORESS. *(Smiling, but with a suggestion of irony)* Alas, such a condition comes only after a long while, and to desire it too strongly does not facilitate its advent. . . . You are of noble birth, my child, and we do not ask that you should forget it. Though you may have renounced the advantages, you cannot escape all the obligations that such an ancestry entails, and here they will seem to you heavier than elsewhere. *(A gesture from Blanche)* Oh yes, you are burning to fill the humblest of positions. Beware of that, too, my child. . . . In wanting to descend too low, one risks overstepping the mark. For an excess of humility, as of anything else, engenders pride, and that pride is a thousand times more subtle and more deadly than that of the world, which more often than not is no more than empty vainglory. *(A silence)* What drives you to enter Carmel?

BLANCHE. Does your Reverence command me to speak quite openly?

THE PRIORESS. Yes.

BLANCHE. Then, the attraction of an heroic life.

THE PRIORESS. The attraction of an heroic life, or that of a certain way of life which, it seems to you — quite wrongly — should render heroism easier, should put it, so to speak, within hand's reach?

BLANCHE. Reverend Mother, forgive me, but I have never made such calculations.

THE PRIORESS. The most perilous of our calculations are those which we call illusions. . . .

BLANCHE. It may be that I have illusions. I should ask nothing better than to be stripped of them.

THE PRIORESS. To be stripped of them. . . . (*She stresses the words*) You will have to take that charge upon yourself alone, my child. Each of us here has already more than enough to do with her own illusions. Do not permit yourself to imagine that the first duty of our calling is to come to each other's aid in order to make ourselves more pleasing in the sight of the Divine Master, like those young women who exchange their powder and their paint before appearing at the ball. Our concern is to pray, as the concern of a lamp is to give light. It would enter no one's mind to light a lamp in order to give light to another lamp. "Each for himself" — such is the law of the world; and ours resembles it a little — "Each for God!" Poor child! You have dreamed of this House like a fearful child whom the servants have just put to bed dreams in its dark room of the sitting-room, of its light and its warmth. You know nothing of the solitude in which a true religious is placed to live and to die. For there is a certain number of true nuns, but there are far more unworthy and faint-hearted ones. Oh yes! Here as elsewhere evil is still evil, and even if made from pure milk, sour cream will turn the stomach just as much as tainted meat. . . . Oh, my child, it is not in accordance with the spirit of Carmel to be moved to pity, but I am old and sick, I am very near my end, and I can well be moved by you. . . . Great trials await you, my daughter. . . .

BLANCHE. What does it matter — if God grants me strength?

Silence.

THE PRIORESS. What He wants to try in you is not your strength but your weakness. . . . *(Silence)* The evil examples that the world provides have the merit of making souls such as yours revolt. Those that you find here will disappoint you. All in all, my daughter, the position of an unworthy nun seems to me more deplorable than that of a brigand. The brigand can be converted and it will be as a second birth for him. The unworthy nun, for her part, cannot be born again. She has been born, but she has missed her birth, and without a miracle she will always remain an abortion.

BLANCHE. Oh, Reverend Mother, I would not wish to see anything here but good. . . .

THE PRIORESS. She who voluntarily blinds herself to her neighbor, under pretext of charity, often does nothing more than to break a mirror so as not to see herself in it. For the weakness of our nature demands that it should be first of all in others that we discover our own wretchedness. Take care not to let yourself be won over by some foolish goodwill or other which will soften the heart and warp the mind. *(Silence)* My daughter, there are many people who ask what purpose we serve; and, after all, their wondering is quite understandable. We think to bring them proof, by virtue of our austerities, that it is perfectly possible to take no heed of many of the things which they consider indispensable. But in order that the example may be effective, it would still be necessary, after all, that they should be sure that those things were once as indispensable to us as to themselves. . . . No, my child, ours is not a profession of mortification, nor are we guardians of virtue; we are a house of prayer, prayer alone justifies our existence, and he who does not believe in prayer can but take us for impostors or parasites. If we were to say so more openly to the ungodly, we should be better understood. Are they not forced to recognize that belief in God is a universal fact? Is it not indeed a strange contradiction that all men can believe in God and yet pray to Him so little and so badly? They rarely do Him more honor than to fear Him. If belief is universal, should it not be likewise with prayer? Well, my child, God wished it to be as it is, not making prayer, at the expense of our freedom, a need as pressing as hunger or thirst, but permitting that some of us should pray on behalf of the others. Thus each prayer, though it be that of a little shepherd-boy keeping his sheep, is the prayer of all mankind. *(A brief silence)* What the little shepherd-boy does from time to time at the urging of his heart, we must do day and night. Not in the least because we hope to pray better than he — on the contrary. That simplicity of the soul, that sweet surrender to the Divine Majesty — which in him is a momentary inspiration, a grace and like to the spark of genius — we consecrate our lives to find or to recover if we have known it, for it is a gift of childhood which more often than not does not outlive childhood.... Once beyond childhood one must suffer to return to it, as at the end of a night one finds another dawn. Have I become a child again . . . ? *(Blanche weeps)* You are weeping?

BLANCHE. I weep less from distress than from joy. Your words are hard, but I feel that even harder words could not break the force which carries me towards you.

THE PRIORESS. It must be tempered without being broken. Believe me, it is an unworthy way of entering our Rule to hurl oneself recklessly into it, like a poor man pursued by thieves.

BLANCHE. In truth, I have no other refuge.

THE PRIORESS. Our Rule is not a refuge. It is not the Rule which protects us, my daughter, it is we who protect the Rule. *(A long silence)* Tell me one thing: have you, by any strange chance, already chosen your Carmelite name, presuming we should admit you as a novice? But no doubt you have never considered it.

BLANCHE. But yes, Reverend Mother. I should like to be called Sister Blanche of the Agony of Christ.

The Prioress starts almost imperceptibly. She seems to hesitate for a moment, her lips move, and then her features suddenly express the firm tranquillity of one who has made her decision.

THE PRIORESS. Go in peace, my daughter.

Scene II

By the door of the close inside the Carmel, some time after. Blanche waits in silence with the Chaplain. She is about to be received as a postulant. The door opens, revealing the whole Community gathered together, each nun wearing the black veil of waist-length, which they raise as soon as the door closes again. The Prioress and Mother Marie of the Incarnation, the sub-Prioress, take the postulant by the hand and, followed by the Community chanting a psalm, lead her to the foot of a small statue representing the Little King of Glory, the child Jesus bearing the royal mantle, the scepter, and the crown.

Scene III

The central corridor of the Carmel, on the first floor. All the cells open on to this feebly-lit corridor. The curfew bell tolls. The Prioress pushes the half-open door of Blanche's cell.

THE PRIORESS. The rule is that doors must be closed, my child. . . .
BLANCHE. I . . . I should have thought. . . . *(With a suspicion of assumed nonchalance in her voice)* The truth is, I cannot see anything at all in here, Reverend Mother.
THE PRIORESS. What do you need to see in there in order to sleep?
BLANCHE. I . . . I . . . I cannot sleep.
THE PRIORESS. The nights in Carmel are short, and a good religious, like a good soldier, should be able to sleep at will. When one is young and in good health as you are, one acquires the habit in course of time.
BLANCHE. I ask your forgiveness, Mother. . . .
THE PRIORESS. Let us forget this childishness.

The Prioress goes out, closing the door. Blanche fumbles in the dark for a moment and finally succeeds in opening the door again. The Prioress returns, notices the door, hesitates, and then goes on her way without closing it.

Scene IV

In the Infirmary. Marie of the Incarnation and the Doctor stand at the Prioress's bedside.

THE DOCTOR. I fear greatly that we can do no more. . . . You have overtaxed your strength, Reverend Mother, and I am not Almighty God. . . .

The Prioress looks at him, then immediately turns her head away and speaks in a reproachful tone and with a rather childish vivacity, in which can be distinguished a fear that she cannot altogether hide.

THE PRIORESS. Indeed? Are you sure? Yet I should have thought . . . Yesterday I ate my soup, not merely without distaste, but almost with pleasure, did I not, Mother Marie of the Incarnation?

MOTHER MARIE. Your Reverence speaks truly.

THE PRIORESS. In truth, I feel much easier than when I had my last attack. The first warm spells of the season have always made me very unwell — that is one of the humors of my constitution which your predecessor, the late M. Lannelongue, knew well. The storm must break, and you will see that by then I am much eased. . . .

The Doctor exchanges a glance with Mother Marie of the Incarnation.

THE DOCTOR. I meant only that it would be well to suspend the use of physics and to let nature take its course, without further disturbing the humors. . . . *Quieta non movere.*

MOTHER MARIE. May God preserve you to us, Reverend Mother . . . !

The Prioress keeps her eyes downcast. The expression on her face is hard. Finally she says, as though to herself:

THE PRIORESS. Into His hands I deliver myself, to find health or to die, according to His Will.

The Doctor goes out with Mother Marie of the Incarnation.

66

Scene V

A corridor outside the Infirmary.

THE DOCTOR. I am sorry thus to have spoken my thoughts aloud in front of the Reverend Prioress. . . .

MOTHER MARIE. Do not be sorry. If you had greater experience of Houses such as this, you would know that there are two kinds of nuns only who can die quite peaceably: the very saintly and the unworthy.

THE DOCTOR. But I should have thought that Faith . . .

MOTHER MARIE. It is not Faith which gives us strength, but Love. And when the Bridegroom Himself comes to us to call us to the sacrifice, as Abraham called his son Isaac, one must be quite perfect or quite foolish not to feel anxiety.

THE DOCTOR. Forgive me. . . . I had thought that in a House of Peace . . .

MOTHER MARIE. Ours is not a House of Peace, Sir. It is a House of Prayer. Those who are consecrated to God do not come together to take pleasure in peace; they try to win it for others. . . . There is no time to take pleasure in what one gives away. . . .

Scene VI

The turn[6] inside the convent near the close. Blanche and a very young Sister, Constance de Saint-Denis, are taking the provisions and everyday articles which the Sister in charge of the turn passes to them.

CONSTANCE. More of these accursed beans!

BLANCHE. They say that the profiteers are holding back the flour and that Paris will lack bread. . . .

CONSTANCE. Look! There is our big iron we have been asking for so long! Look how nicely the handle has been newly covered. . . . We shall not again hear Sister Jeanne of the Divine Childhood blowing on her

6. See note 2, p. 42.

fingers and crying: "Ah-ee! Ah-ee! How can you iron with an iron like this!" Ah-ee! Ah-ee! I have to bite my lip each time so as not to laugh — but I love to hear it! That "Ah-ee" makes me think of the country and the good villagers of Tilly. . . . Oh, Sister Blanche! Six weeks before I entered religion, we celebrated my brother's marriage; all the peasants gathered there, and twenty girls presented him with a garland to the sound of drums and fiddles and a volley of musket-fire. There was high mass, dinner at the chateau, and dancing all day long. I danced five quadrilles — and how I enjoyed them, I can tell you! All those poor people loved me to distraction because I was gay and danced as well as they did. . . .

BLANCHE. Are you not ashamed to talk thus when our Reverend Mother . . . ?

CONSTANCE. Oh, my Sister, if it would save our Reverend Mother's life, I would willingly yield my own wretched little insignificant life, yes, yes, indeed I would. . . . But . . . well, at fifty-nine it is high time to die, is it not?

BLANCHE. Have you never feared death?

CONSTANCE. I do not think so. . . . Yes, perhaps . . . a long time ago, when I did not know what it was.

BLANCHE. And after . . . ?

CONSTANCE. Heavens, Sister Blanche, life suddenly seemed so exciting! I used to tell myself that death must be, too. . . .

BLANCHE. And now?

CONSTANCE. Oh, now I no longer know what I think about death, but life still seems just as exciting to me. I try to do what I am told as well as I can, but I enjoy what I am told to do. . . . After all, am I to be blamed because I enjoy serving God . . . ? It is possible to take very seriously what you enjoy doing — children prove that every day. . . . Exactly as you can do something you dislike with a good grace. . . .

BLANCHE. (In a hard voice) Have you no fear that God may not tire of so much good humor, and may not come to you one day and say to you as to Blessed Angela of Foligno: "It was not for jesting that I loved thee"?

Sister Constance looks at her abashed, her childlike face puckered with distress. Finally she speaks:

CONSTANCE. Forgive me, Sister Blanche. I cannot help thinking that you spoke thus deliberately to hurt me.

Silence.

BLANCHE. Well, you were not mistaken. . . . The truth is, I envy you. . . .

CONSTANCE. You envy me! Goodness, that is certainly the most extraordinary thing I have ever heard! You envy me, when I deserve to be whipped for having spoken so lightly of the death of our Reverend Mother. . . . The death of a Mother Prioress is a very serious matter. . . . I am not used to seeing serious people die. My uncle, the Duc de Lorge, died when he was eighty. But it was not a serious matter — a beautiful ceremony, that was all. My two elder brothers were killed in the war, my first cousin, de Loynes, was killed in a stag-hunt in our own forest of Dampierre, and the other cousin, Jaucourt, whom they called Clair-de-Lune, was drowned in the Mississippi at the time of the American insurrection. . . . All of them died in sport, so to speak. It has always been more or less like that with people of quality. We do not hold the positions we have in the world by virtue of our titles and our rat-gnawed parchment deeds, but by virtue of men for whom death is only a game like any other. . . . Oh. Sister Blanche, since I spoke so foolishly just now, be good enough to help me to repair my fault. Let us kneel and offer our two poor little lives for her Reverence.

BLANCHE. That is mere childishness. . . .

CONSTANCE. Oh no, not in the least, Sister Blanche. I truly believe it is an inspiration of the soul.

BLANCHE. You are laughing at me. . . .

CONSTANCE. The idea came to me suddenly. I do not think it could do any harm. I have always wanted to die young: it cannot be agreeable to have to surrender one's life to God when one no longer wants it, or when one is clinging to it frenziedly only from habit.

BLANCHE. What is my part in this comedy?

CONSTANCE. Well . . . well, the first time I saw you I knew it had been granted to me.

BLANCHE. *(Vehemently)* What had been granted to you?

69

CONSTANCE. I . . . But now you embarrass me, Sister Blanche. . . . You look at me so strangely. . . .

Blanche moves towards her.

BLANCHE. Put down that ridiculous iron and answer me, I beg you.

Constance meekly puts the iron down on the table. Her pretty face is contracted in concern, yet nevertheless retains a kind of childlike serenity.

CONSTANCE. Well . . . I knew that God would grant me the blessing of not allowing me to grow old and that we should die together, on the same day — when and how, I did not know, and at this moment I still do not know. . : . It is what they call a presentiment, nothing more. . . . And now you are so angry with me for attaching so much importance to . . . to . . .
BLANCHE. To an absurd, stupid idea! Are you not ashamed to believe that your life could buy back the life of anyone else? . . . You are as proud as Satan. . . . You . . . you . . . I forbid you . . .

She stops. The expression of rueful surprise on Constance's face gradually fades, as if she were beginning to understand something, though without fully realizing what. . . . She meets Blanche's furious gaze squarely, and it is Blanche who finally drops her eyes. Constance speaks gently, sadly, with a hint of poignant dignity:

CONSTANCE. The last thing I wished was to offend you. . . .

Scene VII

A cell in the Infirmary. Marie of the Incarnation at the Prioress's bedside.

MOTHER MARIE. For some days now she has taken the place of our sacristan. She will be here in a moment.

The Prioress lies in her bed. During the whole scene her movements and her voice contrast with the anguished, almost distracted expression on her face.

THE PRIORESS. Please be kind enough to raise this pillow. . . . Do not you think M. Javelinot would let me be lifted to the armchair? It gives me great distress for my daughters to see me stretched out here as if I had been drowned and my body just brought out of the water, especially since I have kept all my faculties so clear. . . . Oh, it is not that I wish to deceive anyone! But though so miserably lacking in courage, we must at least be capable of appearing composed; else we may be wanting in the respect we owe to those who, out of charity, wish to judge us by our appearance.

MOTHER MARIE. I had understood, Reverend Mother, that your anguish had been much less during the night. . . .

THE PRIORESS. It was no more than an easing of the soul. Nevertheless, God be thanked for it! I no longer felt Death near. "To feel Death near" is taken merely as a saying. Well, Mother, it is true that I feel Death near. Nothing can distract me from that knowledge. Certainly I am conscious of your attentions: I should like to respond to them, but they bring me no succor. You are no more to me than shadows, hardly distinguishable from the pictures and memories of the past. I am alone, Mother, absolutely alone, without consolation. My mind is still quite capable of forming reassuring concepts, but they too are ghosts of concepts. They can bring me no more comfort than the shadow of a leg of mutton on the wall could satisfy hunger. *(Silence)* Speak honestly! If these wretched limbs were not paralyzed and inert, I should scarce believe myself in danger. . . . How many days more does M. Javelinot give me to live?

Mother Marie of the Incarnation kneels beside the bed and gently places her crucifix upon the Prioress's lips.

MOTHER MARIE. Your constitution is one of the strongest he has seen. He fears for you a slow and difficult passing. But God . . .

THE PRIORESS. Even God has become a shadow. . . . Alas! I have been a nun for more than thirty years, and twelve years a Superior. I have meditated upon death each hour of my life, and now it serves me no purpose . . . ! *(A long silence)* It seems to me that Blanche de la Force is very slow to come. *(Silence)* After yesterday's assembly, does she still hold resolutely to the name she has chosen?

MOTHER MARIE. Yes. If it is your pleasure, she still wishes to be known as Sister Blanche of the Agony of Christ. I feel you have always been much touched by this choice?

THE PRIORESS. Yes, for once it was mine. Our Prioress at that time was Mme Arnoult. She was eighty years old. She said to me: "Question your strength. Those who enter upon Gethsemane may not leave it. Have you the courage to remain to the end the prisoner of the Holy Agony?" *(A long silence)* It was I who introduced Sister Blanche of the Agony of Christ into this House. Her well-being is my concern. My wish is to place the matter in order before relinquishing my charge to others. *(Silence)* Of all my daughters, none gives me more anxiety. I had thought of recommending her to your charity. But on reflection, and if God wills it, this shall be my last act as Superior. *(A brief silence)* Mother Marie . . .

MOTHER MARIE. Reverend Mother?

THE PRIORESS. Under obedience, I commit Blanche de la Force to you. You shall answer for her to me in the presence of God.

MOTHER MARIE. Yes, Mother.

THE PRIORESS. You will need great firmness of judgment and character, but that is precisely what she lacks and you have in abundance. *(Silence)* Take care that you do not also need, to carry out your task, to surmount certain feelings natural to you. *(A gesture from Mother Marie)* Oh, I know what I am saying! Where a person such as Blanche is concerned, a person who is in some ways our kin, one's opinion cannot fail to be influenced by certain habits of thinking peculiar to this century, which the religious way of life has been able to discipline but not entirely to suppress. . . .

MOTHER MARIE. *(Hesitates, then openly)* It is only too true. You read me clearly, as always. When our unfortunate nobility, and even Royalty itself, is everywhere slandered, I am ashamed to think that a girl of noble birth could perhaps be lacking in courage.

THE PRIORESS. Yes. When the storm breaks upon this House, it will no doubt fall to others to edify the Community by more precious virtues than our own, but it is to us that the Community may rightly look at least for the example of a certain firmness of mind. No matter! Since our first meeting, when she confessed to me the name she had chosen, Blanche de la Force has stood in my eyes beneath the sign of the Holy Agony. May she remain there for you as well! Ah, Mother, in my present humiliation it is easier for me to understand that the world's code of honor affects the poor daughters of Carmel as the ancient law affected the Lord Jesus Christ and His apostles. We are not here to abolish it, but, on the contrary, to fulfil it while proceeding beyond it.

A knock at the door.

THE PRIORESS. She is there. Ask her to enter.

Mother Marie of the Incarnation goes to the door, steps aside to allow Blanche to enter, and goes out. Blanche comes and kneels by the bed.

THE PRIORESS. Stand up, my daughter. I had intended to talk to you for a longer period, but the conversation I have just had has tired me exceedingly. Do not look at me in that way — the sight before your eyes is a very ordinary one. In Carmel, my child, the difference between the life and the death of a religious should never be marked by more than a change in the times of duties and daily offices. . . .
BLANCHE. Oh, Mother, do not leave me!

Silence.

THE PRIORESS. You are the last-comer here, and because of that the nearest to my heart. Yes, of all my daughters, like the child of parents grown old, the dearest, and also the most exposed, the most threatened. To ward off that threat I would willingly have given my life; yes, indeed I would have given it. . . .

Blanche again throws herself to her knees and sobs. The Prioress places her hand on Blanche's head.

THE PRIORESS. I can now give only my death, a very poor death. . . . *(Silence)* God is glorified in His saints, His heroes, and His martyrs. He is glorified also in the poor.

BLANCHE. I have no fear of poverty.

THE PRIORESS. Oh, there are many kinds of poverty, down to the most wretched, and it is from that kind that you will draw strength. . . . *(Silence)* My child, whatever may come, do not lose your simplicity. One might believe from reading our good books that God tries His saints like a blacksmith tests a bolt to prove its strength. But a tanner also tests a deer-skin between his palms to prove its softness. Oh, my daughter, be ever as soft and as pliable in His hands! The saints did not harden themselves against temptations, they did not revolt against themselves, for revolt is always a tool of the devil. And above all never despise yourself! It is very difficult for us to despise ourselves without offending God in us. And in this respect, too, we should guard ourselves against taking literally certain pronouncements of the saints, for self-contempt can lead straight to despair. Remember my words, for all that they may seem obscure to you now. And to sum up all in a phrase which is never heard upon our lips, though our hearts have not repudiated it: remember that in every circumstance your honor is in the care of God. God has taken your honor in custody, and it is safer in His hands than in yours. Stand up now, for good and all. To God I commit you. God be with you, my little child. . . .

Blanche goes out. Mother Marie of the Incarnation returns with the Doctor.

THE PRIORESS. M. Javelinot, I pray you give me a further dose of that remedy.

M. JAVELINOT. Your Reverence could not support it.

THE PRIORESS. M. Javelinot, you know that it is customary in our Houses for a Prioress to take leave publicly of the Community. This ceremony has been fixed for ten o'clock this morning. On your instructions, I think?

M. JAVELINOT. On my advice, rather. But if I must speak frankly, my art has for many hours now been unable to succor your Reverence more, not even to foretelling with accuracy when the end will come.

MOTHER MARIE. The ceremony of which her Reverence speaks can easily be postponed.

THE PRIORESS. Ah yes, until I am no longer good for anything, no doubt. . . . No, no, Mother. I am confident that God will not abandon me so far that I must leave my daughters without having asked their pardon for a death so different from that of which I should have set the example. Yes, God will grant me that favor. . . . Mother Marie, try to convince M. Javelinot. That elixir or another, no matter which. Oh, Mother, look at me: am I to show this face to my daughters' eyes when soon they come?

MOTHER MARIE. It is perhaps the face of our sweet Lord at Gethsemane.

THE PRIORESS. At least the disciples slept and He was seen only by the angels.

MOTHER MARIE. We do not deserve so much honor, thus through you to discover and to be associated with that which during the Holy Agony was hidden from the eyes of men. . . . Oh, Reverend Mother, do not any more distress yourself on our account. Henceforth concern yourself only with God.

THE PRIORESS. Who am I at this moment, wretched as I am, to concern myself with Him! Let Him first concern Himself with me!

MOTHER MARIE. *(In a voice that is almost hard)* Your Reverence is delirious.

The Prioress's head falls back heavily on her pillow. Almost immediately the death-rattle can be heard.

MOTHER MARIE. Close fast that window. Our Reverend Mother is no longer responsible for what she says, but it is preferable that her words should not scandalize anyone. . . . At this hour the garden is empty, but our Sisters could hear plainly from the washhouse. *(To a young nun who, after shutting the window, comes back trembling)* Come, come, Sister Anne, you are not going to faint now, like some little weakling. Get to your knees and pray. That will do you more good than smelling salts.

75

THE PRIORESS. *(While she speaks, the Prioress sits almost upright. Her eyes are staring, and as soon as she stops speaking her lower jaw drops)* Mother Marie of the Incarnation! Mother Marie . . .

Mother Marie of the Incarnation starts.

MOTHER MARIE. Reverend Mother?

THE PRIORESS. *(In a low, raucous voice)* I have just seen our chapel empty and profaned — oh! oh! — the altar split in two, the holy vessels strewn on the floor, the flagstones covered in straw and blood. . . . Oh! oh! God is deserting us! God has abandoned us!

MOTHER MARIE. Your Reverence is in no condition to restrain your tongue, but I beg her to try not to say anything which might . . .

THE PRIORESS. Not to say anything. . . . Not to say anything. . . . What does it matter what I say! I have no more control over my tongue than over my face. Agony clings to my skin like a waxen mask. . . . Oh, if I could but scratch off that mask with my nails!

MOTHER MARIE. Your Reverence must understand that these are the visions of delirium. . . .

THE PRIORESS. Delirium! Delirium! Have you ever seen this kind of delirium before? Ah, believe me, in this body which lies here like a sack of sand, there is strength to suffer many more days yet.

MOTHER MARIE. Do not prolong any further this struggle against nature.

THE PRIORESS. Struggle against nature! Have I ever done anything else all my life? Do I know how to do anything else? Wretched that I am! After having refused my poor body so much, even the most legitimate of comforts, how should I now yield for the first time to this harassed beast which I can no longer even feel?

MOTHER MARIE. Oh, Reverend Mother, who could not feel compassion for you?

THE PRIORESS. Then may I not first feel compassion for myself?

With a strange cry, she again lets her head fall back on the pillow. Mother Marie bends over her, sees her closed eyes, hesitates a moment, and then quickly rejoins her companions. While she is speaking in a low voice, the

76

Prioress slowly opens her eyes, but does not, however, succeed in suppressing entirely the death-rattle.

MOTHER MARIE. Inform your Sisters that they will not see the Reverend Mother today. At ten o'clock there will be recreation as usual.

The Prioress's eyes have not ceased moving in the face which already seems paralyzed by death. Mother Marie turns round quickly. The gazes of the dying and the living meet. Gradually the sound of the Prioress's death-rattle fades, and finally stops completely — no doubt at the cost of a supreme effort. A long silence. Then the Prioress speaks in a strong voice.

THE PRIORESS. Mother Marie of the Incarnation, in the name of the Holy Obedience, I command you . . .

Scene VIII

The scene suddenly changes. Blanche has just gone to her cell for the night. A bell is tolling. The sounds of moans echo through the convent. It is the Prioress in her death-agony. Blanche, frightened, comes out of her cell and moves towards the light. The Sisters are kneeling outside the Infirmary door. The Prioress can be seen, kneeling erect, supported by nuns, on her bed, but it is difficult to make out what she is saying. Her distorted face turns towards Blanche, and one realizes that she has seen her and is calling her. Almost immediately a Sister comes up to Blanche.

A SISTER. The Reverend Mother wishes you to approach her bed.

Blanche remains stock still as if petrified. Almost roughly the Sister pushes her forward. She moves towards the bed like a sleep-walker.

A change of shot. Now Blanche is by the Prioress's side. Confusion. Several nuns are speaking at the same time. Mother Marie of the Incarnation keeps repeating:

MOTHER MARIE. It is quite senseless. . . . It should not be permitted. . . .

It becomes more and more difficult to support the dying Prioress on her knees. Two kneeling Sisters rise and go to the aid of their colleagues. The Prioress's lips move ceaselessly. Blanche, deathly pale, leans over her several times, but it is obvious that in her distress she can understand little, and the Sisters nearby vie with each other to speak in Blanche's ear the words they have been able to catch: "'Forgive . . . death . . . afraid . . . afraid of death. . . ."' At length, more and more movement is apparent among the group pressing round the dying woman, who, despite all efforts, gradually falls back upon her bed. Blanche, succeeding at last in overcoming her distress, speaks with difficulty.

BLANCHE. The Reverend Mother . . . wishes . . . wishes . . .

Several Sisters say something to her. She breaks off, her face haggard, wondering how to continue, and then says, in tones to which despair has lent a kind of assurance:

BLANCHE. The Reverend Mother . . . wished . . . would have wished . . .

But she falls to her knees, sobbing, her face buried in the sheets of the death-bed.

Scene IX

The convent choir. The body of the late Prioress lies in state in an open coffin, near the grille in the center of the choir. It is night. The choir is lit only by the six candles around the coffin. On either side of the bier is a prie-dieu. Blanche and Constance de Saint-Denis are keeping vigil over the dead woman's body. Reciting of psalms. The flickering flames of the candles light up the Prioress's face eerily. At a given moment, leaving Blanche alone by the bier, Constance goes to call their reliefs. Blanche becomes frightened and runs to the door. There she meets Mother Marie of the Incarnation, who notices her distress.

MOTHER MARIE. What are you doing? Should you not be keeping watch?

BLANCHE. I . . . I . . . Our vigil is over, Mother.

MOTHER MARIE. What do you mean? Are your reliefs in the choir?

BLANCHE. Well . . . Sister Constance went to fetch them . . . So . . .

MOTHER MARIE. So you became frightened and . . .

BLANCHE. I did not think it would be any harm to go as far as the door.

She makes as though to go back, but Mother Marie of the Incarnation says:

MOTHER MARIE. No, my child, no more! Do not go back. . . . A duty left undone is a duty left undone — think of it no more. How you are trembling! But the night is fresh, and I think you shiver less from fright than from cold. I will come with you myself back to your cell.

They are seen outside the cell.

MOTHER MARIE. And now do not brood over this little incident. . . . Go to bed, cross yourself, and sleep. I formally absolve you from all other prayers. Tomorrow your sin will inspire more sorrow than shame in you, and then you will be able to ask God's pardon without offending Him further.

Blanche kneels to kiss her hand. Marie of the Incarnation draws back her hand sharply — a little too sharply perhaps — and closing the door makes a vague gesture of farewell or of benediction.

Part Three

Scene I

The day of the election of the new Prioress. In the convent garden, Blanche and Constance are just completing a cross of flowers for the tomb, which lies beneath the cloisters, of Mme Croissy, the late Prioress.

CONSTANCE. Sister Blanche, I think our cross is quite tall enough and quite broad enough, too. Our poor Mother's tomb is so small!

BLANCHE. What shall we do with the flowers that are left over? Sister Gérald will not want any of them for the chapel. She says a Carmelite chapel is not a repository for Corpus Christi day.

CONSTANCE. Well, we will make them into a bouquet for our new Prioress.

BLANCHE. I wonder whether Mother Marie of the Incarnation likes flowers?

CONSTANCE. Oh! I shall be so happy . . .

BLANCHE. If she likes flowers?

CONSTANCE. No, Sister Blanche — if she is elected Prioress. I've prayed for it so much. God will grant my prayer, I am certain.

BLANCHE. You always think God will act in accordance with your wishes!

CONSTANCE. Why not? After all, Sister Blanche, everyone fashions God as best he can — so why argue about it? There are even people who are unfortunate enough not to believe in Him — I am sorry for them with all my heart, but . . . I hardly dare tell you . . .

BLANCHE. But you will tell me in the end, all the same, Sister Constance. . . . Tell me now.

CONSTANCE. Well, it seems to me sometimes that it is less dreadful not to believe in God at all than to believe in God as a mere mechanic, a mathematician, or a physicist. The astronomers' work has been in vain. I believe that the Creation is as like a piece of mechanism as a real duck at a distance can look like M. Vaucanson's clockwork toy. But the world is not a piece of mechanism any more than Almighty God is a mechanic, or a schoolmaster with his stick, or a judge with his balance. If He is, we should believe that on the Day of Judgment the Lord will seek advice from those who are called serious, balanced, hard-headed people. It is a mad idea, Sister Blanche! You know well that that kind of people have always thought the saints to be fools, and the saints are the true friends and counsellors of God. . . . So . . .

BLANCHE. So?

CONSTANCE. So, in my belief, with all due respect for the serious people, God is perfectly capable of letting Mother Marie be elected simply to please a poor little worm such as I. It would be madness, no doubt, but He committed a much greater madness in dying on the Cross for my sake!

BLANCHE. I prefer to think that Mother Marie will be elected because she is the most worthy.

CONSTANCE. Oh! I may be young, but I well know that good fortune and misfortune seem to be dispensed at hazard rather than shared out logically! But perhaps what we call chance is the logic of God? Consider the death of our dear Mother, Sister Blanche! Who would have believed that she would have found death so hard, that she would know so little how to die! One would say that just as He was giving it to her, God mistook her death, as one is given the wrong surcoat from a cloakroom. Yes, that must have been someone else's death, a death which did not fit our Prioress, too small for her, so that she could not even get her arms into the sleeves. . . .

BLANCHE. Someone else's death — but what, in fact, does that mean, Sister Constance?

CONSTANCE. It means that this other person, when the hour of death comes, will be surprised to find it so easy, to find death comfortable. . . . Perhaps she will even boast of it: 'See how at ease I am — how well the skirt falls. . . .' *(Silence)* We do not die each for ourselves, but each for another, or even each in place of another, who knows?

Silence.

BLANCHE. *(In a voice which trembles slightly)* Look, our bouquet is finished. . . .
CONSTANCE. And suppose we should have made it for Mother Marie of St. Augustine . . . ?
BLANCHE. What are you thinking now, Sister Constance!
CONSTANCE. Oh, no doubt at any other time no one would have considered Mme Lidoine. But some of our Sisters say that Mother Saint Augustine would be better liked by the townsfolk, because her father was a cattle-dealer at Caumont. Faith! Things are going from bad to worse, it seems, Sister Blanche! And Mme Lidoine believes that one should cut one's losses.

Scene II

As the bell rings, the Community assembles in the chapter-house for the ceremony of allegiance to the new Prioress. She is Mme Lidoine, Sister Marie of Saint Augustine. Like all the communal rooms, this one is small and vaulted. On one wall hangs a very fine crucifix. Beneath it is the Prioress's chair. Along the walls are benches where the nuns are sitting. The ceremony of allegiance. Each religious comes and kneels before the Prioress and kisses her hand. The new Prioress gives a short address:

THE PRIORESS. . . . My dear daughters, I must furthermore tell you that we find ourselves deprived of our much-lamented Mother at a time when we need her presence most. We have without doubt come to the end of the prosperous and peaceful times when we forgot too readily that nothing assures our safety, that we are always in God's hands. What the years we are going to live in will mean to us, I do not know. I look to Holy Providence for only the modest virtues which the rich and powerful so readily hold in contempt — goodwill, patience, the spirit of conciliation. More than for others, they are suitable for poor daughters like us. For there are many kinds of courage, and that of the great men of the earth is not that of the little men, for they could not bear it. The valet must possess only certain of the master's qualities — they do not all agree with him any more than thyme and marjoram agree with our tame rabbits. A man who is quite certain of never offending God can bear with a lot, whatever the cost to his self-esteem. "Barking dogs don't bite" — empty words, and bad reasoning; more things are achieved by persuasion than force, and a drop of honey will catch more flies than a pint of vinegar. I repeat, we are poor daughters gathered together to pray to God. Let us shun anything which may turn us from prayer, let us even shun martyrdom. Prayer is a duty, martyrdom a reward. When, in the presence of all his court, a great King calls his maidservant to come and sit beside him on his throne, like a well-beloved bride, it is better for her, at first, not to believe her eyes or her ears, and to continue to scrub the floor. I ask your forgiveness for my rather homely mode of expressing myself. Mother Marie of the Incarnation, perhaps you will bring this little talk to an end. . . .

Hesitation. But Mother Marie is not one who must be asked the same thing twice.

MOTHER MARIE. My Sisters, her Reverence has just told us that our first duty is prayer. But that of obedience is not less important, and should be carried out in the same spirit; that is to say, with a complete disregard for our own feelings and our own judgment. Let us then follow not only with our lips but with our hearts her Reverence's wishes.

Scene III

The Prioress's cell. She has received a letter from Mgr Rigaud, the Superior of the Carmel, asking her to give the veil to the postulants.

MOTHER MARIE. With your Reverence's permission, and in all sincer-
ity, I cannot approve this taking of the veil.

THE PRIORESS. Sister Blanche is a postulant, and Mgr Rigaud asks me
to give the veil to the postulants — that is the crux of the problem.

MOTHER MARIE. If your Reverence puts it in that way, she solves the
problem in advance.

Silence.

THE PRIORESS. Are you not afraid you may be taking childish actions
too seriously? Without wishing to offend you, Mother Marie, I spent
all my youth among girls who did not believe themselves dishonored if
they were frightened by ghosts, or even by rats or mice. Nevertheless,
they later grew into women who were sticklers for duty, hard-headed
housewives who could make their presence felt. In your noble families
a slightly timorous girl looks upon herself straightway as a wart in the
middle of a face! Why yes! A person of quality's reputation is as deli-
cate as those skins which cannot bear the sun's rays. . . . What do they
matter to us, these mincing ways? By my head! Carmel is not an order
of chivalry, when all is said and done!

MOTHER MARIE. Your Reverence is perhaps more right than she
thinks. There are refinements on points of honor which are more than
nonsense. But for all this fear of rats or mice, those girls of whom you
spoke did not lack character, to judge by what they later became. It is in
character that Blanche de la Force is wanting.

THE PRIORESS. How can you talk so of a religious whose hand our
Reverend Mother wished to clasp as she died and whom she entrusted
to you?

MOTHER MARIE. My sympathy for Blanche de la Force cannot prevent
me from assuring your Reverence that in the trials that threaten us that
lack of character may prove perilous to the Community.

Silence.

THE PRIORESS. Mgr Rigaud wishes this taking of the veil. . . .

MOTHER MARIE. It is difficult not to defer to that wish, I confess. But in the event that your Reverence decides upon it, I should wish her permission henceforth to give help, by special acts of penitence, to . . .

A gesture from the Prioress. Silence.

MOTHER MARIE. Naturally I should wish nothing better than to solicit your Reverence's agreement on each occasion. . . .

THE PRIORESS. Oh, let it be as you will, Mother. We seem rather unlike, our paths are not exactly similar, and yet we shall always understand each other very well, if God pleases. . . . Your fears are justified, I do not pretend otherwise. But let me take in my hands this little aristocrat, as it is the fashion to say nowadays, and I will make a true Carmelite of her for you, as good in the chapel as in the washhouse, a wise Virgin incapable of losing her head, even in ecstasy, for it was so that our Holy Foundress wished her daughters to be, was it not? Ah yes! My comparison just now was not so foolish — I know my people. In France you need not scratch a girl of noble birth for long to discover the peasant beneath, and the haughtiest duchess enjoys the same health of body and soul as her dairymaid. . . .

MOTHER MARIE. Your Reverence is certainly capable of forming my daughter as she says, but I fear she lacks the time.

Scene IV

The Ceremony of Blanche's taking of the veil in the convent choir. The Sisters wear long veils and white cloaks. The altar is covered in flowers. Blanche is also in white, but her face is not veiled. The new Prioress and Mother Marie of the Incarnation lead her to the grille. She receives the name of Blanche of the Agony of Christ.

Scene V

The visiting-room. A delegate of the municipality and the convent notary explain that they have to take an inventory of the Community's possessions,

85

which are now placed at the disposal of the Nation. This inventory concerns all the land belonging to the convent and the dowries brought by the Sisters on entering religion. The tone of the proceedings is perfectly courteous, and the registrars ask for pardon for their action.

Scene VI

Recreation after this visit and the taking of the inventory.

THE PRIORESS. . . . You know what this proceeding by the registrars means. I would say that we are threatened with poverty, if poverty could ever be a threat to us. What are you whispering, Sister Blanche?

BLANCHE. My Reverend Mother, I was saying . . . I was saying: all the better! We will work.

THE PRIORESS. If you were in our place, my child, you would know that the difficulty is to exist in poverty without offending the decencies. Our business is not to prove to passers-by that one can live without eating, like Père Mathieu's famous ass, who died the same day he was going to show that he could. And what would you work at, Sister Blanche?

BLANCHE. We could undertake dressmaking, Reverend Mother. . . .

THE PRIORESS. Let us first see what resources we have before working out our future means. Sister Mathilde, what is there left of our winter provisions? Since her Reverence's death, I must confess that I have not set foot in the storehouse. . . .

SISTER MATHILDE. There is not a great deal left, Reverend Mother. The hard frosts went on into the middle of March, and towards the end of her life the Reverend Mother tended to give without counting the cost. Counting was not her strong point.

THE PRIORESS. It is mine. Listen, my daughters, too often until now we have lived like fine people who are in a position to squander their money right and left. What use would it be to give comfort to a few more beggars if we bring ruin upon our House, so that next winter the poor people should find our doors closed . . . ? In faith, it would be the

86

story of killing the goose that laid the golden eggs all over again. . . . Come, Sister Blanche, I can see that we shall have to return to your dressmaking.

BLANCHE. It would be so diverting!

THE PRIORESS. Sister Blanche's fingers are itching at the mere thought of handling lawn and lace once more. . . .

SISTER MATHILDE. Without meaning to reproach you, Sister Blanche, it will be less tiring than sawing wood like we have been doing since Wednesday, Sister Anne and I. . . .

THE PRIORESS. Come, come, my daughters, your task cannot irk you so much. I hear you laughing all the time.

SISTER ANNE. That is because it reminds us of our homes, Reverend Mother. Sister Mathilde and I are almost neighbors. She comes from Cormeilles and I from Blémont-sur-Oise.

SISTER MATHILDE. Heavens, we are not afraid of work.

THE PRIORESS. Peace, peace, my little children! No boasting! I will wager that in your homes the girls still had an easy time of it. Your father has bought almost all the lands of his overlord, and the Marquis de Manerville is now much poorer than his farmer. . . .

Sister Blanche is standing a little apart. A Sister takes a few steps towards her, away from the group, and cries:

SISTER GERTRUDE. Upon my soul, Reverend Mother, Sister Blanche seems to be weeping!

She brings Blanche back. Blanche forces herself to smile.

SISTER MATHILDE. We were jesting, Sister Blanche. It is our place to saw wood, and it gives us a good appetite.

THE PRIORESS. What a frivolous conversation, to be sure! Would you not say that the spirit of the age penetrates everywhere, even through the walls of the convent!

SISTER MARTHE. There are neither bourgeois nor aristocrats here.

THE PRIORESS. Ah — good intentions, but foolish words!

SISTER MARTHE. I crave your Reverence's forgiveness. I meant only that we are all sisters. And should not all men be brothers likewise? Have we not been made equal in Holy Baptism?

SISTER VALENTINE OF THE CROSS. Brothers are not necessarily equal among themselves, Sister Marthe. . . .

SISTER MARTHE. Perhaps not.

SISTER ALICE. But the nobles are not our elder brothers, Sister Valentine of the Cross. You know well the old saying: "When Adam delved and Eve span, who was then the gentleman?"

SISTER VALENTINE OF THE CROSS. Not so fast, Sister Alice! They say that our first father lived for more than a thousand years. We can wager that before he died he must certainly have indicated from among so many children those who would till the ground, and those, a much smaller number, who would defend it against robbers. And so gentlemen were born.

SISTER MARTHE. The fact that sheep gave their wool before anyone thought of training dogs to guard them should not be held against the sheep, nor against the dogs, nor against the shepherd.

SISTER ALICE. It has been known for a dog to make a meal of a sheep.

SISTER VALENTINE OF THE CROSS. If the sheep rid themselves of the dogs, would they be the better protected against the wolves for it?

SISTER ANNE. It is true that it is the nobility who fight our wars. Our overlord has lost three sons in the King's service, and his father was quite crippled from a musket-shot in the kidneys. Now the Demoiselle is an old maid because she has no dowry. It is heart-breaking to see M. le Comte at Mass on Sundays with his breeches all patched.

SISTER ALICE. But I would wager he carries his nose in the air, none the less.

SISTER MATHILDE. If he chose not to now, he would have chosen a poor time to change.

SISTER MARTHE. Yes, that is true, Sister Mathilde, we must be fair. My good father is not without means, but he is just a simple villager like any other. That does not prevent him from being appalled at the sight of drunkards and good-for-nothings lording it about, people who never do any honest work except at harvest-time.

SISTER VALENTINE OF THE CROSS. The "patriots" have burned nine châteaux in the Beauvoisis alone.

SISTER ALICE. Oh yes, Sister. But think how like epidemics of the plague or cholera are times of great trouble. They bring out the rabble everywhere like rain brings out snails and slugs. All the same, there are some "patriots" who honor Christ. In Verchin they say that they carried the Cross of our Lord in triumph.

SISTER VALENTINE OF THE CROSS. After having pillaged the church and cut off the heads of the saints of the portal . . .

SISTER ALICE. Verchin is but a wretched little village, and we should not base our opinions on what happens there.

SISTER GERTRUDE. That is true, Sister Alice. Verchin is Verchin, but Paris is Paris. . . . And was it not in Paris that our good King presided at that famous celebration when the Lord Bishop of Autun officiated on a platform twenty feet high? Did not our Chaplain tell us then that no such spectacle had been seen since Roman history began?

CONSTANCE. (Bursting out) What do we want with Greeks and Romans? What have we French to learn from anyone?

SISTER GERTRUDE. You are in fighting mood all of a sudden, Sister Constance. . . . Are you going to work at Sister Blanche's dressmaking with a helmet on your head and a sword at your side?

CONSTANCE. Oh, you can laugh, Sister Gertrude. It does not matter. If my sex and my position allowed it, I would give a good account of myself to these people of whom you speak. . . .

SISTER GERTRUDE. When you see them close up, my little Sister . . .

CONSTANCE. I shall not give a fig for them.

SISTER GERTRUDE. Take care, my little Sister. St. Peter was well punished for speaking like you.

CONSTANCE. Oh, St. Peter . . . ! St. Peter . . . To begin with, St. Peter was neither a Frenchman nor a . . . (She stops short)

SISTER GERTRUDE. Nor what, then?

SISTER ALICE. Speak boldly, Sister Constance. . . .

SISTER MARTHE. Let us wager she was about to say that St. Peter was not a gentleman.

They all laugh.

SISTER ANNE. How will you get out of that, Sister Constance?

SISTER MARTHE. Is it true? Yes or no?

CONSTANCE *(Incapable of lying)* It is true that that was my thought. *(Entreating them, with tears in her eyes)* But I did not think thus out of pride, or with contempt for anyone. I meant only that since St. Peter was not a soldier he was wrong to give our Lord a soldier's word. . . . He was a simple fisherman. If he had merely given his fisherman's word, he would have kept to it.

BLANCHE. Well answered, Sister Constance!

SISTER GERTRUDE. Oh you, Sister Blanche . . . !

A very short silence, just long enough to indicate that there is in the convent a certain feeling of distrust of Sister Blanche. But a Sister immediately speaks to dispel the embarrassment they all feel.

SISTER MARTHE. And what do you think of the "patriots," Sister Blanche?

The brief silence has obviously disconcerted Blanche. She has gone pale and her lips tremble.

BLANCHE. I . . . I . . . I think they have little love for religion, my Sister. . . .

SISTER MARTHE. Perhaps they are ignorant of it . . . ?

SISTER VALENTINE OF THE CROSS. Oh! Oh! You have great illusions, my Sister. . . .

SISTER MARTHE. And you little prejudices, my Sister. . . .

THE PRIORESS. Come, come, my children! We slacken the reins for ten minutes and you are already, God forgive me, arguing among yourselves like their Lordships in the High Judicial Courts! Let this humiliating experience be a lesson to those who think themselves quite cut off from the world because they find it pleasant to pray. You see, my daughters, the people think us very different from them. Yet our holy Rule and this House — no less dependent one upon the other than the body and the soul — are like the regal majesty or the sumptuous vestments which sometimes mask the wretchedness of a tainted body. Away from the Rule and our House, what would become of us, poor wretches? You may be certain then that no price will be too high for me to make sure that we are allowed to live here, according to our vocation, though the rest of the world be in flames. Before fighting violence, the spirit of our Rule commands that we should first do all we can to disarm it; just as there is no warfare without deaths, there is no martyrdom without murder, and a humble daughter of Carmel should consider that, unless she cannot avoid it without offending Almighty God, it is a very costly means of winning our glory for poor handmaids like us to do so, perhaps, at the risk of the eternal salvation of our executioners. . . . And besides, why talk of martyrdom? There is no question of martyrdom for us, and I do not wish you to become excited by such thoughts. We risk being thrown into the streets, that is all. We are in the same situation as the poor who have not been able to pay off the midsummer quarter and find themselves without a penny at Michaelmas. There is something to cool your imaginations for you.

Scene VII

The Prioress is with Marie of the Incarnation. A doorbell rings. Sounds are heard, muffled by the thickness of the walls. The Prioress and Marie of the Incarnation look at each other questioningly. At last a Sister enters.

THE PRIORESS. What is happening?

A SISTER. There is a man on horseback at the wicket-gate, asking to see the Reverend Prioress.

THE PRIORESS. At which wicket-gate?

A SISTER. The one in the lane.

THE PRIORESS. If he takes so much trouble to avoid being seen, he cannot be an enemy. Go and see, Mother Marie.

The Reverend Mother is standing, and her lips move almost imperceptibly. But her face remains impassive. After a moment Mother Marie returns.

MOTHER MARIE. Reverend Mother, it is M. de la Force, who wishes to see his sister before he leaves for foreign parts.

THE PRIORESS. Let someone go and inform Blanche de la Force. The circumstances authorize this infraction of the Rule. But I desire you to be present at the interview.

MOTHER MARIE. If your Reverence would be good enough to allow . . .

THE PRIORESS. You, Mother Marie, not any other.

Scene VIII

The parlor. The curtain is drawn half-way. Blanche's face is not veiled. Behind the drawn curtain, Mother Marie of the Incarnation, wearing the long veil, is present.

THE CHEVALIER. Why have you been sitting like this for twenty minutes, your eyes downcast, scarce replying? Is this the welcome due to a brother?

BLANCHE. Heaven knows how little I wish to displease you in any way!

THE CHEVALIER. The long and the short of it is that our father feels you are no longer safe here.

BLANCHE. Perhaps I am not, but I feel safe — that is enough for me.

THE CHEVALIER. How different is your tone from what it used to be. There is something restrained and forced in your manner now.

BLANCHE. What you take for restraint is no more than lack of habit and awkwardness. I have not yet accustomed myself to living happily and free from bondage.

THE CHEVALIER. Happily perhaps, but not free from bondage. It is not within your power to conquer nature.

BLANCHE. What, does the life of a Carmelite seem to you so much in conformity with nature!

THE CHEVALIER. In times like these there is more than one woman, once envied, who would willingly change her position for yours. I am speaking harshly to you, Blanche, but in truth I have before my eyes the vision of our father, deserted but for the servants.

BLANCHE. (*With a gesture of despair*) You believe that fear keeps me here!

THE CHEVALIER. Or fear of fear. That fear is no more honorable, after

92

all, than any other. One must be able to risk fear as one risks death —
true courage lies in taking that risk. But perhaps I speak too roughly
for you, too like a soldier? God is my witness that I have never ceased
to see in you an innocent victim of the most cruel, the most unjust of
fates. . . .

BLANCHE. *(In a choking voice)* Henceforth I am here in the hands of
the Divine Majesty. God will act with me as He wills.

THE CHEVALIER. Without being a Sorbonne theologian, I would reply that it would be likewise here or elsewhere.

BLANCHE. No, my brother, it is here that I feel myself most at His
mercy.

THE CHEVALIER. That kind of conviction cannot absolve you from
obeying your father's wishes.

BLANCHE. In taking the veil, I have ceased to depend on him. I owe
him only my love and my heartfelt respect.

THE CHEVALIER. Blanche, when I came in just now, you were very
near swooning, and in the light of this poor lamp, in one moment I
thought to see again the whole of our childhood. It is probably through
my clumsiness that we have come almost to throwing challenges at
each other. Have they changed my little hare?

BLANCHE. They have changed her. Oh, not, of course, in her affection
for you! But it is true that the wonderful day when I took the veil was
like to a second birth.

THE CHEVALIER. If I understand you aright, this second birth releases
you from all obligations towards him to whom you owe the first? Oh,
Blanche, have done with idle hairsplitting! Remember that our friends
and relations are dispersed; no one here would stop you going to rejoin
our father. He can count on none but you.

BLANCHE. Do you not remain to him?

THE CHEVALIER. My duty calls me to the army of M. le Prince.

BLANCHE. Well, mine holds me here. Oh, why do you wish to instill
doubt in me like a poison? I all but perished once from that same poison. It is true that I am altered. It is true that God has given me the
quality of strength, that gift of the Holy Spirit of which I am unworthy,
but which, nevertheless, is a thousand times more precious than the
carnal courage on which men pride themselves so much.

THE CHEVALIER. You are no longer afraid of anything!

BLANCHE. I know that you are mocking me. Yet it is true that I no longer fear anything. Where I am, nothing can reach me.

A silence.

THE CHEVALIER. Then, farewell, my dear.

She has suddenly drawn nearer. As he says "farewell," she falters and grasps the grille with both hands. Her voice changes in tone, though she tries to keep it firm.

BLANCHE. Oh, do not leave me with an angry farewell! Alas, you have looked upon me with compassion for so long that now you find it difficult to substitute for it the simple respect that you would feel, almost without thinking of it, for any of your friends!

THE CHEVALIER. Blanche, now it is you who speak harshly.

BLANCHE. I have naught for you but gentleness and affection. But I am no longer your little hare. I am a daughter of Carmel who is to suffer on your behalf, and of whom I should like to ask you to think as a companion in arms, for each of us will fight after our own fashion, and mine has its risks and its perils just as yours.

She speaks these words with the slightest of childish emphasis and awkwardness which make them the more touching. Marie of the Incarnation has taken a step forward. The Chevalier looks at Blanche for a long while, but without revealing his thoughts. Blanche clings to the grille so as not to fall. Mother Marie of the Incarnation comes forward.

MOTHER MARIE. Compose yourself, Sister Blanche.

BLANCHE. Oh, Mother Marie, have I not lied? Do I not know myself for what I am? Alas, I was so harassed by their pity! God forgive me! The kindness of it sickened my soul. Oh, shall I never be more than a child in their eyes?

MOTHER MARIE. Come, it is time to go.

BLANCHE. I have been proud, and I shall be punished.

MOTHER MARIE. There is only one means of conquering pride: to raise oneself above it. But one should not contort oneself in an effort to become humble, like a cat trying to force itself into a rat-hole. True humility is first of all a propriety, a balance. *(As she goes, she gently straightens Blanche's bowed figure)* Hold yourself proudly.

Scene IX

The Chaplain arrives as the interview ends, and invites the Chevalier to supper before he continues his journey. He takes him to his quarters and himself serves the meal.

THE CHAPLAIN. To speak frankly, M. le Chevalier, I believe your sister is better here for the present where God wants her.

THE CHEVALIER. Oh, we have never thought of forcing her to leave. I have for her, as well as the most tender affection, the kind of feeling that a man as simple as I must experience towards a being marked out by destiny. She came into the world laden with all the gifts of birth, fortune, and nature. Life was for her like a cup filled to the brim with a delicious liquor that turned to gall as soon as she put her lips to it.

THE CHAPLAIN. Come, come, we have said all we need to say about it. Return to this little wine instead — it is as pure as gold and as fresh as spring-water. It will be your stirrup-cup. What do you propose to do now?

THE CHEVALIER. To set off well before dawn. For the road is not safe until Vermont. But there I have a hiding place where I may gather my strength a little and send a despatch to my father.

THE CHAPLAIN. He must, indeed, be alarmed for your safety.

THE CHEVALIER. It is I who am alarmed for his. For, old though he is, nothing affects his good humor nor alters his habits. You would say that in denying themselves nothing, the survivors of those generations which were made for pleasure have learned to dispense with all. He watches events follow one another like the trunks of trees swirling in a flood, and believes he may leave matters until the river has returned to its bed.

THE CHAPLAIN. Alas! I very much fear that before the river returns to its course it will have carried away its banks. When you return, M. le Chevalier, how much will you find of what you left to defend?

THE CHEVALIER. Bah! The torrent will break down only that which bars its way. What have you to fear?

THE CHAPLAIN. My son, the French have never fought amongst themselves except on behalf of and to the benefit of others. But they have always wished to believe that they were fighting for principles. So each civil war becomes a religious war.

THE CHEVALIER. But their only grudge is against the nobility.

THE CHAPLAIN. Nonsense! It is you who are feared, but it is we who are hated. . . .

Scene X

A commission comes to the convent, led by a strange little man wearing the cap of Liberty. Marie of the Incarnation accompanies him.

A COMMISSARY. What means this nonsense?

MOTHER MARIE. Simply that this Sister must precede you ringing the bell. Such is the rule in this House.

FIRST COMMISSARY. We know no other rule than the Law. We are the representatives of the Law.

MOTHER MARIE. We are but poor servants of our Law. That must excuse my insistence. But since you are in a position to exact what is refused to you, I will insist no more.

A COMMISSARY. To business, quickly!

MOTHER MARIE. I wish to keep you as little as possible. Our Reverend Mother Prioress has given me orders to conduct you over this House.

A COMMISSARY. We shall make our inspection just as well without you.

MOTHER MARIE. My role is not to keep company with you, but to spare you the trouble of forcing locks that I can open with my keys.

ANOTHER COMMISSARY. Let us not argue with her, citoyen. She's a sly cat — she'll always have the last word.

FIRST COMMISSARY. I pray you, citoyen, to use language more suited to the mission which is entrusted to us.

MOTHER MARIE. If you ever in truth expected to find here gold or arms, as they say in the journals, is it not enough that you have searched our little cellar and our storeroom from top to bottom? What good is there in visiting now the cells, where you will find only a mattress and a prie-dieu?

FIRST COMMISSARY. Perhaps we shall also find some young citoyennes, who, confined here by their families, are in need of the Law's protection.

Mother Marie opens the door of the first cell. It is empty. She opens a second door, which closes behind her. The sound of voices is heard. The door again opens, and a nun appears. Her face is almost hidden by the long veil.

FIRST COMMISSARY. I insist that you make an end of this ridiculous masquerade. Raise that veil.

The religious remains motionless. Mother Marie gently tells her to raise the veil. She is a very old nun, who bears no resemblance to the conception of a young girl "confined here by her family." The Commissary loses patience.

FIRST COMMISSARY. Citoyenne, give me your keys. This citoyen will himself let me into the cells. Your presence undoubtedly overawes these wretched women.

The dwarf opens the door of Blanche's cell. As soon as his twisted features appear in the crack of the door, Blanche screams piercingly; her hands outstretched, she backs to the wall at the rear of the cell, and remains pressing herself against the wall as if she were awaiting death. Mother Marie remains in the corridor. Her face sharply betrays a first reaction, which no doubt is impossible to conceal, of contempt and anger at Blanche's cowardice. The door shuts behind the Commissaries. The sound of voices inside. Mother Marie visibly controls her feelings and remains without moving. The door again opens.

FIRST COMMISSARY. Citoyenne, I charge you to tell me how long this young person has been confined here.

MOTHER MARIE. I think, sir, that you should ask her yourself.

FIRST COMMISSARY. It seems she has lost the use of her tongue.

MOTHER MARIE. Do you not think that you, Sir, may have terrified her in entering her cell? Do you not consider that your appearance and your behavior are calculated to distress her?

ANOTHER COMMISSARY. Citoyen Monstrelet, do not be taken in by her wiles. The young citoyenne shall explain it straightway before the Municipality.

MOTHER MARIE. Your search-warrant gives you no right of arrest. That girl will not leave here except of her own free will.

She goes into the cell. Though outwardly quite calm, a trace of anxiety mingled with pity is apparent in her expression.

MOTHER MARIE. Sister Blanche . . .

FIRST COMMISSARY. I forbid you to continue. . . .

MOTHER MARIE. You have the power to force me to silence, but none to command me to it. I represent here the Reverend Mother Prioress, and I shall take no orders from you.

A COMMISSARY. Confounded old hag! She can't be made to hold her tongue, citoyen, but remind her that the Republic has a machine at its disposal that will leave her somewhat short of breath!

FIRST COMMISSARY. Enough! I repeat that you must behave as a true representative of the people. *(He turns to Blanche)* Young citoyenne, you have nothing to fear from us who are your liberators. Say but one word and you will find yourself beyond the sway of those who, the better to put you in their power, have not feared to offend against nature in usurping even the sacred name of Mother. Henceforth you are under the protection of the Law.

MOTHER MARIE. But first she is under my protection. Do you think I shall permit you to take any further advantage of a child's terror? I shall take great care to avoid a language that you cannot understand. Of that which holds us here and keeps us here united unto death, you know nothing, or if once you knew it, it is now doubtless forgotten. But there are still perhaps words which are common to us and which can touch your conscience. Well, sir, you must know that to the poorest daughter of Carmel honor speaks louder than fear.

At the word "honor," Blanche raises her eyelids. She looks from one to the other, as if she were just waking. She throws herself, sobbing, into the arms of Marie of the Incarnation.

Scene XI

Before the chapter-house, the door of which is guarded by two soldiers. The Sisters are assembled under the cloisters and are called inside one by one, there to undergo interrogation. Before entering each one kneels before the Prioress and asks her blessing. When Mother Marie's turn comes she kneels like the others, then goes into the chapter-house. The Commissaries are standing about the room; their leader sits nonchalantly in the Prioress's chair. Marie of the Incarnation remains standing.

THE COMMISSARY. For the time being we must rest content with the declarations that the citoyenne has just made. But do not think that the matter is closed, so far as she is concerned. I shall report what I have seen to the Municipality.

MOTHER MARIE. It is to your conscience, sir, that you will have to report. I hope for its sake that you will soon find before you some other adversary than a terrified child.

THE COMMISSARY. What adversary? You perhaps?

MOTHER MARIE. I could be an adversary to no one.

THE COMMISSARY. But I am your adversary.

MOTHER MARIE. Perhaps that does not depend on you, for my duty and my preference are in accordance in refuting you as such.

THE COMMISSARY. I know I shall not get the vantage of your impudence.

MOTHER MARIE. I shall content myself with giving you no opportunity to exercise yours. For the rest, it should be enough for you to know that I am entirely at your mercy.

THE COMMISSARY. You speak in that tone with the sole intent of subjecting to your power once more a spirit as weak as yours is strong, indeed inflexible.

MOTHER MARIE. That is true. You are not mistaken.

THE COMMISSARY. As long as there are people such as you, there will
be no safety for the patriots.

MOTHER MARIE. Yet we ask no more than to live in freedom, according to the rule we have chosen.

THE COMMISSARY. There is no liberty for the enemies of Liberty.

MOTHER MARIE. Our liberty is beyond your reach.

THE COMMISSARY. Of what use would it be to have taken the Bastille
if the nation tolerates other bastilles such as this, a thousand times
more despicable, for it is not to despotism but to superstition and lies
that innocent victims are sacrificed here each day? Yes, this house is a
bastille, and we shall destroy the vile den.

MOTHER MARIE. Do not omit to destroy us, too, to the last one. Where
there is a daughter of St. Teresa, there is a Carmel. . . . Come, Blanche.

*For a moment Blanche has been looking at her with a kind of naïve admi-
ration and complete, childish confidence. She follows her like a shadow.*

Scene XII

*The convent chapel. The Chaplain in priestly vestments finishes saying
Mass and comes back from the altar. He approaches the grille and calls the
Sisters to come nearer.*

THE CHAPLAIN. My dear daughters, what I have to say is no longer
a secret to some of you, and the others will scarce be surprised. I have
been relieved of my functions and proscribed. The Mass I have just
said is my last. The tabernacle is empty. I repeat today the gestures
and also no doubt the words of our first Christian fathers, of our fathers in Christendom, at each new persecution. In the affairs of the
world, you know, when all hope of conciliation is gone, force is the
last resource. But our wisdom is not of this world. In the affairs of
God, the last resource is the sacrifice of consecrated souls. At all
times God never ceases to call them to him, but today one might say
that he calls them by name. This is a day of splendor for Carmel.

Farewell. I give you my blessing. We will sing together the Adoration of the Cross.

As he goes he blows out the sanctuary lamp and leaves the tabernacle door open.

Scene XIII

The parlor. Blanche and the Chaplain on either side of the grille.

BLANCHE. What will become of you?

THE CHAPLAIN. I shall remain as I am at this very moment, a proscribed priest.

BLANCHE. They say "an outlaw."

THE CHAPLAIN. My poor child, a fish cannot live out of the water, but a Christian may well live outside the law. What does the law guarantee to us? Our goods and our life — goods which we have renounced, a life which no longer belongs to any but God. . . . That is as much as to say that the law has little value for us.

BLANCHE. But if the stories they tell are true, they will kill you if they recognize you.

THE CHAPLAIN. Perhaps they will not recognize me.

BLANCHE. You will disguise yourself?

THE CHAPLAIN. Yes. Such are the orders we have received. Dear Sister Blanche, your imagination always becomes inflamed too swiftly. The unhappy men who threaten us have more hatred than cunning, and it may well be that I shall soon be rid of them, thanks to a few precautions which I shall soon be in the habit of taking, just as you will.

BLANCHE. Just as we shall? You are not leaving us?

THE CHAPLAIN. Yes, my child. Set your mind at ease. I shall stay near this House, and I shall come here as often as possible. It is something we shall have to plan, and we shall arrange it all, Mother Marie and I.

Silence.

BLANCHE. Oh, what must Mother Marie think of me? I am so unworthy of her kindness.

THE CHAPLAIN. One is always unworthy of what one receives, my child, for one never receives anything except from God. Remain at peace. It is not breaking a secret to say that since the death of our Reverend Prioress the charity of Mother Marie has covered you with its shadow — *obumbrabit tibi* — to speak like the psalm, you should continue to hope beneath her wings — *sub pennis ejus sperabis*. I know that Mother Marie has answered for you before God.

Scene XIV

Blanche, when she leaves him, runs to Marie of the Incarnation.

BLANCHE. Oh, Mother Marie, is it true? Have you, indeed, answered for me before God?

MOTHER MARIE. How can you talk like that? Each one answers for himself, my daughter. But it is true that our Reverend Mother Prioress confided you to me as she was dying.

BLANCHE. I am a heavy enough charge for you.

MOTHER MARIE. And also a light one. The charge of a child is never heavy, but it gives much cause for concern.

BLANCHE. It seems to me that I shall give you hardly any more, I feel so confident when I am with you, Mother!

MOTHER MARIE. Do not rely on any but God for your strength, my little daughter.

Scene XV

The garden. Some of the Sisters are picking fruit. Constance has climbed into one of the trees and is eating the fruit.

SISTER MATHILDE. Anxiety has caused you no loss of appetite, Sister Constance. But my basket is scarce becoming filled that way.

CONSTANCE. What do we need with so many provisions? Perhaps we shall be dead before the fruit has time to molder.

SISTER MATHILDE. And supposing we do not die at all. I certainly have no great wish to die, Sister Constance.

CONSTANCE. Oh, neither have I! But if we leave it to God whether we shall die or not, why should we trouble ourselves whether we shall eat or not? We shall never again have such an opportunity to be a little greedy!

SISTER MATHILDE. That is a strange way to prepare yourself for martyrdom!

CONSTANCE. Oh, excuse me, Sister Mathilde. In chapel, at work, and during the times of silence, I can indeed prepare myself in a different way. This is the way of recreation. Why should they not both be good ways? And anyway, when all is said and done, the function of martyrs is not to eat but to be eaten.

Scene XVI

The Prioress's cell. The Prioress shows Marie of the Incarnation the decree which prohibits the taking of vows by nuns. The Prioress is seated. Marie of the Incarnation, standing, finishes reading the decree.

MOTHER MARIE. Is it credible that a government could make itself so ridiculous as to prohibit the taking of vows?

THE PRIORESS. Credible or not, the decree must be quite clear to you.

MOTHER MARIE. Has your Reverence decided to conform to it?

THE PRIORESS. Yes.

MOTHER MARIE. Then Sister Constance and Sister Blanche will not be able . . .

THE PRIORESS. No.

Silence.

MOTHER MARIE. Has your Reverence considered that Mlle de la Force will thus be deprived of a very necessary consolation and comfort?

THE PRIORESS. I have considered it. I cannot risk the security of all my daughters for the sake of Mlle de la Force.

MOTHER MARIE. Not for the sake of Mlle de la Force perhaps, but for the sake of the last wishes of a dead woman and for the honor of the Community.

THE PRIORESS. For one of us to fail will be only a trial and a humiliation. Mother Marie, I do not wish to say anything to embarrass you, but you speak of honor as though we had not long ago renounced the esteem of the world. You know very well that it is in the shame and ignominy of His Passion that the daughters of Carmel follow their Master.

MOTHER MARIE. Have they not first been present in the solitude and terror of His last night? Would it not be a dread misfortune for us all to see that very one of us fail who bears indeed the name of the Holy Agony? In a battle it is to the bravest that the honor of bearing the standard is given. It seems as though God wished to put ours into the hands of the weakest and perhaps least worthy. Is it not like a sign from Heaven?

THE PRIORESS. I fear that sign is given to you alone. It is you, my daughter, who will be sacrificed to that weakness and perhaps substituted for the contempt.

MOTHER MARIE. I shall agree to it with all my heart.

A long silence.

THE PRIORESS. You see, Mother Marie, a ceremony like that is never so secret that something of it does not become known, sooner or later, in a town filled with spies. The least indiscretion would end in our throats being cut.

MOTHER MARIE. What can we wish for better than to die?

Part Four

Scene I

The chapter-house. All the Sisters are ceremoniously assembled. Before reading the decree, the Prioress recites with her daughters the hymn of St. Teresa of Avila:

> *I am Thine, and born for Thee:*
> *What wilt Thou have done with me?*
> *Give me poverty or wealth,*
> *Comfort me or make me sad,*
> *Chasten me or make me glad,*
> *Send me Hell or grant me Heaven.*
> *Sun, with veil for ever riven,*
> *I have yielded all to Thee:*
> *How wilt Thou have done with me?*[7]

THE PRIORESS. I must read to you the decree of the Assembly which prohibits the taking of religious vows until further notice. "Decree dated October 28th, 1789. The National Assembly decrees that the offering of monastic vows shall be suspended in all religious houses, for either sex,

---

7. From the translation by E. Allison Peers, *The Complete Works of Saint Teresa of Jesus*, vol. 2 (London: Sheed and Ward, 1946).

and that the present decree shall be enacted pursuant to the royal sanc-
tion and disseminated to all tribunals and to all monasteries." Such a
measure must sadden all of us, but it affects cruelly indeed our Sisters
Constance and Blanche. So it is to you two that I shall speak first, my
dear daughters. I ask you to make generously this sacrifice of the happiness which you have waited for. In the secret of your hearts you will offer
to His Divine Majesty the vows that a cruel order forbids you to pronounce ceremoniously. That the order is unjust is not for us poor serv-
ing-maids to consider, for our vocation is in no way to oppose ourselves
to injustice, but simply to atone for it, to pay the ransom; and since we
possess nothing but our wretched persons, we are ourselves that ransom.
Since we do not oppose ourselves to injustice, neither have we any right
to judge its instruments. In our thoughts as in our prayers those who per-
secute us cannot be distinguished from the poverty-stricken, or may be
distinguished only by a greater poverty — to put it more clearly, by the
most extreme wretchedness imaginable, for they seem to be deprived of
God's grace to such a point that they believe themselves His enemies.
Such poverty cannot be eased with soup, however good; it is prayers
which it needs, and the tradition of Carmel is to provide prayer of irre-
proachable quality. That should keep us in true modesty. For in all
knowledge of the duties of my charge, I must tell you that I shall no longer tolerate a certain exaltation which — high though its motives may be
— distracts us, none the less, from the humble duties of our position.
There is more childishness than evil in it, I know, but to put an end to
this nonsense nothing is more necessary than to point out its contradic-
tions, if not even its absurdity. What! You think to pray for sinners, that
is, for their conversion or their betterment, and at the same time you
hope to see them commit the gravest of murders — against consecrated
persons? Let us speak frankly! A Carmelite who desires martyrdom is as
poor a Carmelite as a soldier who seeks death before having carried out
the orders of his commander. But an end to proverbs and comparisons.
My considered wish is that this community should continue to live as
simply as in the past. The convents have so far been spared, and there is
nothing to prove that they will not be spared in the future. In addition,
whatever may happen, let us count only on that kind of courage which
God dispenses day by day — as it were, drop by drop. That courage is fit-

ting to us, and is best suited to the humility of our position. And yet it is
perhaps too great a presumption to ask it of Him. It would be better to
pray to Him humbly that fear shall not try us beyond our strength, that
we shall feel only its humiliation, without being forced to some blame-
worthy action. Remembering the Garden of Gethsemane, where in the
Adorable Heart of our Lord the whole of human anguish was made Divine, the distinction between fear and courage seems to me of little im-
port, and fear and courage both seem to us like the gewgaws of luxury.

Scene II

*The Community disperses. One group goes to the garden, where Blanche
joins Marie of the Incarnation.*

BLANCHE. Mother Marie, is it possible that her Reverence refuses to
grant us, even at such a time as this, the consolation of pronouncing
our vows in clandestine? We know well that if the decision were yours .
. .
MOTHER MARIE. I too can do nothing but obey.
BLANCHE. But her Reverence has so much faith in your judgment. . . .
MOTHER MARIE. My duty is to have more faith in her judgment than
in mine.
BLANCHE. But our taking of the veil . . .
MOTHER MARIE. At that time we were merely threatened with an im-
minent law. Today we fall under a law in force, and her Reverence has
every reason to wish not to arouse unnecessarily our enemies' anger.
BLANCHE. Is it indeed you, Mother Marie, who speaks thus? Have we
reached such a state of misfortune that our only hope is to pass unnoticed like a hare in its form?

Scene III

*The singing of the Carmagnole can be heard outside the convent, and the
Commissaries, followed by the crowd, still singing, burst into the close.*

They break down the door of the convent. Preceded by a Sister ringing the little bell, they invade the sacristy, heap the ornaments and holy vessels in the turn, which they have broken open, and cover the whole with the veil from the grille. They strip the Little King of Glory of His mantle and crown, and throw the statue into a corner. The Prioress is present during the pillage, but the Community has gathered in the chapter-house. Led by Mother Marie of the Incarnation, they offer up prayers. Each wears the long veil.

MOTHER MARIE. Come, come, my sisters, be calm! For the moment there is no other prayer possible than that. Remain in true accord with God.

When the door opens before the Prioress, they stay motionless. One head only turns in fright — that of Blanche.

THE PRIORESS. Silence! I will not tolerate my House becoming like an overturned antheap. *(Silence)* Of all that saddens our souls today, we must deplore only the sacrilege and pray for those who commit it. As for the gold or the silver that they steal, what does it matter? Is not our first rule that of poverty? Poor as we may be henceforth, we still follow our Master only from afar; we are still not as poor as He. *(Gradually the restless atmosphere changes to calm)* Come, come! It is not the first time that churches and convents have been pillaged. It has been known often enough in the course of wars.

Scene IV

The cell of Mother Jeanne of the Childhood of Jesus, a very old nun. Outside snow is falling. Mother Jeanne finishes sewing a mantle, of very poor quality, for the Little King of Glory. Blanche helps her to reclothe the statue in it.

MOTHER JEANNE. My little Sister Blanche, you know that on Christmas Eve our Little King is carried to each cell. I pray He will bring you courage.

Scene V

Christmas Eve. The corridor in the convent, all the cell doors open. The Prioress and Mother Marie of the Incarnation, accompanied by two Sisters bearing torches, take the Little King from cell to cell. Each nun kneels to receive the statue, clad in its poor robe, places it on the ground, venerates it, and returns it to the Prioress, who kneels in her turn.

SISTER ANNE. Our Little King has become as poor again as He was at Bethlehem.

When the Little King is presented to Blanche, she starts and murmurs, with tears in her eyes:

BLANCHE. Oh, how small He is! How weak He is!
MOTHER MARIE. No! How small He is — but how powerful He is!

As Blanche, kneeling, receives the statue, the song of the Carmagnole resounds outside the convent walls. Blanche trembles, allows the Little King of Glory to slip from her fingers, and the head of the statue shatters against the flagstones. Terrified, with the expression of a stigmatist, Blanche cries out:

BLANCHE. Oh! The Little King is no more! Now we have only the Lamb of God.

Scene VI

The Prioress's cell. Blanche has just entered.

THE PRIORESS. My daughter, let us first kneel and say together the prayer of our Mother St. Teresa.

The Prioress recites each phrase of the prayer and Blanche immediately repeats it after her.

THE PRIORESS, *then* BLANCHE.
> I am Thine, and born for Thee:
> What wilt Thou have done with me?
> Give me poverty or wealth,
> Comfort me or make me sad,
> Chasten me or make me glad,
> Send me Hell or grant me Heaven.
> Sun, with veil for ever riven,

But Blanche changes the ending of the prayer.

THE PRIORESS.
> I have yielded all to Thee:
> How wilt Thou have done with me?

BLANCHE.
> Give me refuge or mortal anguish:
> How wilt Thou have done with me?

The Prioress looks at her, hesitates a moment, and finally pretends to have noticed nothing. They get up. The Prioress sits. Silence. Then:

THE PRIORESS. I suppose you know why I have called you here?

Silence. Blanche drops her head, without replying.

THE PRIORESS. The separation will be no less hard for the mother than for the child. *(Silence)* I do not wish to act otherwise than with your agreement, my daughter, or at least with the agreement of your conscience. I do not ask you to reply to what I am going to say; or if you reply, it will be later and to God alone, in the recollection of prayer. My daughter, neither you nor I can hope more deeply that you will succeed in overcoming your mortal anguish.... *(Silence)* No doubt, in other times ... or later ... perhaps ...

Silence. Blanche looks at the Prioress in distress, with an almost wild expression. It is obvious that the Prioress is affected by Blanche's pain, though her face hardly betrays it. However, her voice trembles as she says:

110

THE PRIORESS. Do you indeed believe that we are doing you a wrong in sending you back into the world?

For a moment Blanche is silent. Then she makes a great effort to reply:

BLANCHE. I . . . It is true that I no longer have any hope of surmounting my nature. No . . . I no longer have any hope. . . . Oh, Reverend Mother, anywhere else I must drag my shame as a convict his ball and chain. This House is indeed the only place where I may hope to offer it to the Divine Majesty, like a sick man his shameful sores. For, after all, Reverend Mother, perhaps God wishes me to be cowardly just as He wishes others to be good or to be stupid. . . . *(She sobs)*
THE PRIORESS. Do not distress yourself. I will think further of all this.

Blanche kneels and kisses the hand of the Prioress, who blesses her.

Scene VII

Clandestine celebration of Good Friday, in a dependent building of the convent, where some of the faithful have met together. It is night and some of the men are keeping watch. Women and children are present. The nuns arrive noiselessly, and one of them prepares the holy vessels. The priest has not yet come.

One or two words given in signal are heard outside. . . . The priest enters, and some of the children kiss his hand.

THE CHAPLAIN. When I left you for the first time, I hoped to see you again often. But the circumstances have been very far from those I foresaw. I can say that they render my ministry more difficult each day. Henceforth each of our meetings will come about only at the pleasure of God, and we should thank Him for them as for miracles. What, then, of that? In less sombre times, homage to the Divine Majesty can easily take on the character of a simple ceremonial, too like that which is observed in honor of the princes of this world. I do not say that God does not accept that kind of homage, though the spirit which inspires it is more in accordance with the Old Testament than with the New. But it may be that He grows weary of it, if you will allow the expression. Our Lord lived and always lives among us in poverty, and the moment always comes when He decides to make us as poor as He, so that He may be received and honored by the poor, in the way of the poor, so that He may rediscover thus what He knew formerly so many times on the roads of Galilee — the hospitality of the poverty-stricken, their simple welcome. He wished to live among the poor; He also wished to die with them. For it was not as a Prince at the head of his train that He went to His death, that is to say, Jerusalem, the place of His sacrifice, in those dark days which preceded the first Easter. It was among poor people who, far from thinking to be defiant, made themselves small in order to pass unnoticed for as long as possible. . . . Let us also make ourselves small, not, like them, in order to escape death, but to suffer, if it so happens, as He Himself suffered, for He was truly, in the words of the Holy Scriptures, a lamb led to the slaughter. Now let us proceed to the Adoration of the Cross.

The priest goes, after having promised the Sisters that he will return on Easter Day.

Scene VIII

Easter morning. The priest is awaited.

THE PRIORESS. That was not the Chaplain?

MOTHER MARIE. No, Reverend Mother, and it is now so late that I fear he will not come.

THE PRIORESS. Has watch been kept along the lane? Remember, he has tried once already to return by the washhouse door, but it was locked.

SISTER GERTRUDE. Sister Antoine has been on guard there since dawn.

SISTER ANNE. It seems they came yesterday evening to fetch our old baker, Thibaut, to take him before the Municipality.

SISTER MARTHE. It was his rival, Serval, who denounced him.

THE PRIORESS. *(Still calm)* I know, I know. . . . But since Friday evening the Chaplain has had a new hiding place.

CONSTANCE. Is it credible that in a Christian country people allow their priests to be hunted? Are the French such cowards now?

SISTER MATHILDE. They are afraid. Everyone is afraid. They pass their fear on to each other, like the plague or cholera in an epidemic.

SISTER VALENTINE OF THE CROSS. How shameful!

BLANCHE. *(As if despite herself, in an almost toneless voice such as those one hears in dreams)* Perhaps fear is, in fact, an illness.

A slight murmur, then silence. Blanche seems to awake, glances right and left to meet the veiled looks, which, however, show embarrassment rather than reprobation.

MOTHER MARIE. We do not feel fear; we imagine we feel fear. Fear is a phantasm of the devil.

BLANCHE. *(In the same strange voice)* And courage?

MOTHER MARIE. Courage, too, may well be a phantasm of the devil. Another one. Thus each of us may have to struggle with our courage or our fear like a madman playing with his shadow. One thing alone matters, that, brave or cowardly, we should always be where God wishes us to be, trusting in Him for everything else. Yes, there is no other cure for fear than to throw oneself body and soul into God's mercy, like a stag pursued by the hounds plunges into running water.

CONSTANCE. But a stag at bay ends by turning on the hounds. Are there no good Frenchmen to come to the defence of our priests?

THE PRIORESS. That is not our concern.

MOTHER MARIE. *(To the other Sisters)* Her Reverence does not mean, however, that we may not hope for it.

SISTER ALICE. What purpose shall we serve when, because there are no priests, our people are deprived of the sacraments?

THE PRIORESS. When there are no priests there are martyrs in abundance, and so the balance of Grace is readjusted.

Silence. It can be seen that Mother Marie is about to speak, but she still hesitates. Some of the Sisters have quickly turned their heads towards her. In the end, all gaze at her, except Constance and Blanche. Blanche keeps her eyes downcast, with an expression of desperate sadness on her face. Constance watches her with a kind of burning curiosity.

MOTHER MARIE. *(Suddenly, in a low urgent tone, which reveals all the intensity of feeling behind it)* It seems to me that the Holy Ghost has just spoken through the lips of her Reverence.

General reaction. Silence. The Prioress maintains an impassive face, but one senses that her forbearance is strained. A dramatic atmosphere, which reveals a glimpse of the deep dissension between the two women.

MOTHER MARIE. *(In the same urgent tones)* I think the entire Community should, by pronouncing solemnly the vow of martyrdom, answer this impious regime which tries to prohibit the taking of vows.

General reaction, though restrained, of agreement. Two or three old nuns bow their heads. Blanche slowly raises hers and gazes anxiously at Mother Marie of the Incarnation.

MOTHER MARIE. That France may still have priests, the daughters of the Carmel have nothing more to offer but their lives.
THE PRIORESS. *(Coldly, after a long silence)* You must have misheard me, Mother, or at least you misunderstood me. It is not for us to decide whether or not our wretched names shall appear later in the breviary. I should never wish to be among those guests of whom the Gospel speaks, who take the first place and risk being sent to the last by the Master of the Feast.

Mother Marie keeps a respectful silence. The faces of certain young Sisters show disappointment and some even contempt.

THE PRIORESS. Come . . . come. . . . The name of "martyr" is easily said. But if that misfortune were to overtake us . . .

MOTHER MARIE. *(As if despite herself)* Your Reverence would surely not call it a misfortune to . . .

THE PRIORESS. I use the word in its ordinary sense. I speak a common, day-by-day language. There have been great saints who have rejoiced in death, others who have abhorred it, and some who have even fled from it. By my head! If we are to call good fortune what ordinary men call misfortune, shall we be the better for it? To wish for death while in good health is to fill our souls with emptiness, like a madman who thinks to feed on the smell of roasting meat.

She watches her daughters for a moment, particularly the young ones, peering over her spectacles. They have all lowered their heads. The Prioress's look and voice soften strangely.

THE PRIORESS. I needed to steady you a little, my daughters. Your feet were no longer on the ground; you were becoming so light that a puff of wind in your skirts would have been enough to raise you to the skies and to lose you in the clouds, like M. Pilatre's balloon. . . . And I have great need of my daughters! What should I be without my daughters? An old woman — rather down-to-earth, something of a chatterbox, as you have just heard . . .

A silence. The atmosphere becomes calmer.

THE PRIORESS. Mother Marie, God is my witness that my words then were not meant for you. And there will never be better occasion than this to say, here and now, what I think: you deserve this charge a thousand times more than I; but as long as I hold it, I shall act in accordance with my common sense and my nature, for I believe that Providence had its reasons for giving the Community, in such grave circumstances, as simple and as unworthy a Superior as I.

MOTHER MARIE. Your Reverence knows that nothing is more pleasing to me than to conform in my judgment with yours.

THE PRIORESS. Were you in my place, it would be a great happiness for me, too, to pronounce this vow of martyrdom, and to pronounce it beneath your guidance. . . .

MOTHER MARIE. Your Reverence may be assured that the whole Community . . .

THE PRIORESS. There is no "whole Community." A Community always has its strength and its weakness; the strength and the weakness are each as necessary as the other. It is in consideration of these weaker elements that I cannot give the authorization you wish.

Two or three Sisters have instinctively turned towards Blanche, and immediately they turn back. Blanche's head slowly inclines more and more, but she does not appear to realize this. Constance is very pale; she mutters a few words.

THE PRIORESS. *(With great gentleness)* What are you saying, Sister Constance? I willingly give you leave to speak. When the wise have come to the end of their wisdom, it is right to listen to the children.

CONSTANCE. Is that your Reverence's command?

THE PRIORESS. Very well — yes!

CONSTANCE. I should like to ask the Community pardon for being among the weaker ones of whom your Reverence has just spoken.

THE PRIORESS. Are you so sure of that?

CONSTANCE. With your Reverence's permission . . .

During this dialogue Blanche has raised her head. At the moment when Sister Constance begins to speak again her eyes meet those of Blanche. For a moment Sister Constance hesitates to continue. It should be apparent that the compassion she feels for her friend cannot, however, force her to lie; she overcomes the difficulty by an equivocation, to which her first conversation with Blanche, at the beginning of the film, gives meaning. She is more and more pale, but resolute.

CONSTANCE. With your Reverence's permission. It is true that I am not absolutely certain that I am afraid to die, but I love life so much! In the end, is it not the same thing?

SISTER ANNE. Sister Constance takes no heed of a word that she speaks. . . .

SISTER GERTRUDE. You scandalize us, Sister Constance!

116

CONSTANCE. *(Without thinking)* What do I care? *(She stops short, the blood mounting to her cheeks)* I ask your pardon, my Sister. I meant that in speaking as I have just done, I had resigned myself in advance to being despised, that is all.

THE PRIORESS. No one here thinks of despising you, Sister Constance — rather do you edify us. *(A silence. Then with a smile of understanding, almost of complicity)* But one should not court contempt any more than martyrdom. Each thing comes in its own good time.

Scene IX

The workroom. Some of the Sisters are dressmaking. They are discussing the Chaplain's sermon.

SISTER VALENTINE OF THE CROSS. I have never heard such a sermon!

SISTER ALICE. Perhaps that is because you have never heard the Passion preached by a priest himself in peril of death.

SISTER CLAIRE. Death. . . . It is difficult in the face of death to envisage the Master of Life and Death.

SISTER MARTHE. In the Garden of Olives, Christ was no longer master of anything. Human anguish had never risen to such heights; it will never reach that level again. It had claimed all of Him except that extreme part of the soul where the Divine acceptation was concentrated.

SISTER CLAIRE. He was afraid of death. So many martyrs have not been afraid of death.

SISTER GÉRALD. Not only martyrs — brigands also. Thus Cartouche jested while he was being broken on the wheel, so they say.

SISTER ST. CHARLES. Oh yes, indeed! Her Reverence is right. The heroism of martyrs and the other kind are like gold and copper. One is precious, the other common, but none the less they are both metals.

SISTER CLAIRE. The martyrs were sustained by Christ, but Christ had no one's aid, for all succor and mercy proceed from Him. No living soul enters death so alone or unarmed.

SISTER MATHILDE. The most innocent is still a sinner and he feels confusedly that he deserves death as such. The most criminal replies only for his own crimes, while He . . .

SISTER CATHERINE. The most innocent and the most criminal, having committed no sin, but responsible for all sin, devoured by justice and injustice at the same time, as if by two ferocious beasts. . . .

SISTER GERTRUDE. Oh, Sister Catherine, you make my blood freeze. . . .

SISTER CATHERINE. And you, Sister Gertrude, how will you spend your last night as a person condemned?

SISTER GERTRUDE. In faith, it seems to me the occasion will appear to me so splendid that my fear of being unworthy of it will triumph over my fear of it.

SISTER ANNE. And I should like to mount the scaffold first. I should go quickly towards the guillotine without looking to right or to left, as I used to do at home climbing the big ladder, so that my head should not reel.

SISTER GERTRUDE. And what would you say at that moment, Sister Constance?

CONSTANCE. I? Oh, nothing at all!

SISTER GERTRUDE. What, not even a prayer?

CONSTANCE. I know not. My good angel would say it for me. I shall have enough to do to die *(with a quick veiled look at Sister Blanche).* And, anyway, are you not ashamed to excite yourselves like this?

SISTER GERTRUDE. Heavens, it is not a crime! Better to pass the time in chatter than in sighing.

SISTER VALENTINE OF THE CROSS. And you, Sister Blanche?

Hearing her name, Blanche seems to awaken with a start. The cloth and the scissors in her lap fall to the ground. She picks them up, but says nothing.

SISTER FÉLICITÉ. Well, Sister Blanche, what is the matter with you?

SISTER CLAIRE. Leave Blanche de la Force in peace. Do you not see she was drowsing?

SISTER FÉLICITÉ. Blanche de la Force. . . . Without wishing to be unkind, Sister Blanche, you should rather be called Blanche de la Faiblesse. . . . Come, tell us what you would think if they took you to prison.

Blanche tries unsuccessfully to steady her voice.

BLANCHE. To prison. . . . Well, Sister Félicité, I . . . I . . .
SISTER FÉLICITÉ. Come, tell us!
BLANCHE. *(In a childish voice)* In faith. . . . Well, I should be afraid to be quite alone, to be without our Mother.

Smiles. Out of charity heads are turned away. Sister Constance keeps her eyes on the floor, but one senses that she is struggling with anger. A Sister appears suddenly.

SISTER ANTOINE. My Sisters, our Reverend Mother is coming to bid you farewell.

The Prioress, called to Paris by her superiors, appears in lay clothes.

Scene X

The convent garden. As usual, a very happy atmosphere.

SISTER GERTRUDE. Recreation is lasting longer than usual today.
SISTER CATHERINE. Not at all. We still have a good twenty minutes, Sister Gertrude.
SISTER ST. CHARLES. We have never enjoyed ourselves so much as since her Reverence left. What would she think of us!
SISTER MARTHE. Was it not her Reverence herself who recommended us to be joyful and carefree so long as God allows us this respite?
SISTER ANNE. Respite! You might as well speak of respite to a man hanging on a wire a hundred feet above the cathedral square!
CONSTANCE. *(Laughing)* But we, my Sister, can only fall into God's hands.
SISTER ANNE. Oh, Sister Constance, what an edifying remark! Why did you speak it laughingly?
CONSTANCE. Because it gives me pleasure to think of it.

SISTER ANNE. Ha! When our Reverend Mother came to bid us farewell, did you not laugh then, too?

CONSTANCE. That was because Sister Alice prodded me in the middle
with her elbow. But I should have laughed all the same. I laughed to
see our Reverend Mother in so fine a get-up.

SISTER GERTRUDE. Were you not ashamed?

CONSTANCE. And why should I have been ashamed? I think it is very
laughable that the wicked should only succeed in forcing the poor servants of God to disguise themselves as if it were a carnival.

SISTER VALENTINE OF THE CROSS. They will not stop at that.

CONSTANCE. And after that? What will they do more than Nero or
Tiberius? Was not the disguise of all disguises the ignominious death
of our Lord? They disguised the Master of all Creation as a slave and
nailed Him to the wood as a slave; Earth and Hell together have not
capped that monstrous sacrilegious jest. To feed men to the beasts or to
transform them into blazing torches — does it not suggest some horrible farce? Oh, no doubt suffering and death always astonish us, but in
the sight of the Angels, what can these inhumanities signify? No doubt
they would laugh at them, if Angels could laugh. . . .

SISTER GERTRUDE. Sister Constance defends herself well. . . .

SISTER VALENTINE OF THE CROSS. Oh, you, Sister Gertrude —
you listen with your mouth open to everything she says.

*They turn to Sister Gertrude. A general burst of laughter. Her mouth is,
in fact, open, her head is on one side, her eyes half-closed, like someone
who is listening very attentively. The confusion of laughter and voices
continues for a moment, and then dies by degrees. Silence. The boom of a
distant bell is heard. Then another, nearer. Yet another. The Sisters look
at each other.*

SISTER MATHILDE. The tocsin!

SISTER ALICE. Cannon-fire!

SISTER ANNE. How can it be cannon-fire? Why should it be cannon-
fire? It must be the great bell of St. Maxime's chapel.

SISTER ALICE. Impossible, Sister Anne! The sound comes from over
there. . . .

Indeed the cannon can now be heard quite clearly. The blaring of trumpets. The sounds of a marching crowd. The Ça Ira. . . . Festive songs.

SISTER CLAIRE. *(Dully)* It reminds me of Corpus Christi in the old days.
SISTER ST. CHARLES. Oh, be quiet! Be quiet!

She falters. A nervous laugh is heard. The blaring of the trumpets now drowns all other noise. But between each blast there is a brief moment of silence. In one of these pauses the little turn-bell sounds.

SISTER MATHILDE. Someone has rung the bell!
SISTER CLAIRE. We must see at once if there is someone at the wash-house door.

Sister Anne hurries off.

SISTER CLAIRE. Take care, Sister Anne! Do not unchain the door unless you are certain!

Almost immediately the Chaplain rushes in. They surround him. A Sister stands a few paces away and keeps watch on the great door. The footsteps of a marching crowd.

THE CHAPLAIN. I was almost trapped between the crowd and a patrol. I had no recourse but to return here.
SISTER CLAIRE. Stay with us, Father.
THE CHAPLAIN. I cannot compromise you. I must leave. When the procession has reassembled in the market-square, the streets will be free.
CONSTANCE. But will there never be any remedy but to flee or to hide?
THE CHAPLAIN. In troubled times such as these the worst risk is not to be a criminal but to be innocent, or merely suspected of being innocent. The innocent will soon pay for the whole world!
SISTER CATHERINE. Oh, Father, leave this country!
THE CHAPLAIN. I shall wait to learn God's pleasure on that score. In staying where He has placed me, I may commit a foolishness but not a sin.

SISTER CLAIRE. What will become of her Reverence?

THE CHAPLAIN. I know not. I fear that she will not be able to return to us.

The trumpets are still blaring, but apparently they are no longer on the move.

SISTER MATHILDE. I think the street is empty now, but it sounds as though another procession is forming beside the cathedral. Is that not so, Sister Anne?

SISTER ANNE. Yes. The old gardener has just come to fetch his clothes. He says that the town is full of strangers who are going to camp for the night in the squares. They are selling wine at every crossroads.

SISTER FÉLICITÉ. Listen! Listen!

The tocsin, which had momentarily stopped, is resumed even louder. Now gunshots can be heard.

SISTER VALENTINE OF THE CROSS. In faith! Only a quarter of an hour ago we were so confident, so calm. . . .

SISTER MARTHE. Bah, Sister Valentine! There has been enough noise in the town since this morning.

SISTER VALENTINE OF THE CROSS. No more than usual. The town has been mad for so many days. Yesterday, did they not dance all the night by the water's edge? We could hear the fiddles from here. And there were sudden gunshots, which made one think of midsummer fireworks.

SISTER MARTHE. It is true that in the end one notices none of it. . . .

SISTER FÉLICITÉ. Listen! There they are again.

THE CHAPLAIN. Perhaps I have tarried too long. No matter!

SISTER CLAIRE. Do not leave without giving us your blessing.

THE CHAPLAIN. I should like to take leave of Mother Marie of the Incarnation.

SISTER ANNE. After dinner our Mother Marie of the Incarnation retired to her cell, as is her habit.

SISTER CLAIRE. Go and find her, Sister St. Charles.

122

THE CHAPLAIN. No. It will be better not to waste time. What would become of you, my daughters, if they should find me in your house?

He prepares to bless them. They kneel. He blesses them and then disappears. Almost immediately the noise redoubles in the main street. It sounds as if the street had suddenly filled with an immense crowd.

The Chaplain has climbed the wall of the adjacent garden, in which there is a toolshed. He stays hidden there until nightfall. The noise increases ceaselessly, to a point where the Sisters, to make themselves heard, have to shout into each other's ears. Blows begin to rain upon the door.

A FEW PANIC-STRICKEN VOICES. Do not open! Do not open!

The first reaction of the Sisters is to run up and down in the little garden. But one after another, as if ashamed, they calm down. At last they gather at the foot of the statue of the Virgin. It is apparent why when the silhouette of Mother Marie of the Incarnation is seen at the top of the little flight of steps outside the chapel door. A plank in the outer door has just given way with a sinister crack. Mother Marie of the Incarnation signs to Sister Constance and takes from her bunch of keys the key of the great door, which she hands to Constance.

MOTHER MARIE. Go and open it, my little daughter.

One guesses the words from the movements of her lips rather than hears them. The noise is now quite deafening. The door is broken in. Mother Marie of the Incarnation moves forward, without haste, neither too quickly nor too slowly. Two or three revolutionaries climb through the breach, but they do so only by means of a kind of acrobatics which makes them look ridiculous, and they stop for a moment, rather embarrassed in front of the motionless Sisters. Mother Marie gently takes the key from Constance's hand and holds it out to one of the three men. The door is opened. The crowd bursts in. Mother Marie of the Incarnation has made no move to restrain them, and yet most of the invaders cross back over the threshold. Sister Constance is very pale, but an almost imperceptible smile can be seen on her lips.

A COMMISSARY. Where are the nuns?

MOTHER MARIE. You see them there.

THE COMMISSARY. Our duty is to acquaint them with the decree of expulsion.

MOTHER MARIE. That duty rests with you.

The reading of the decree.

"Whereas it has been decided by the Legislative Assembly, sitting August 17th, 1792.

"From the 1st October next all houses still currently occupied by religious of either sex shall be evacuated by the said religious and shall be put up for sale at the suit of the administrative bodies."

THE COMMISSARY. Have you any claim to make?

MOTHER MARIE. What could we claim, since we no longer possess anything? But it is imperative that you should procure us some other clothes, since you forbid us those we wear now.

THE COMMISSARY. As you wish. *(Forcing himself to banter, for the great simplicity of Mother Marie's bearing overawes him)* Are you in so great a hurry then to quit these cast-offs and to dress yourselves like anyone else?

MOTHER MARIE. I could well reply that it is not the uniform which makes the soldier. But we have no uniform. In any habit, we shall never be but servants.

THE COMMISSARY. The people have no need of servants.

MOTHER MARIE. But they have great need of martyrs, and that is a service we can undertake.

THE COMMISSARY. Bah! In times like these it is nothing to die.

MOTHER MARIE. To live is nothing, that is what you mean. For death alone counts when life is brought to ridicule, and has no more value than your assignats.

THE COMMISSARY. Those words could cost you dear if you uttered them before another than I. Do you take me for one of those vampires? I was sacristan in the parish of Chelles. The Curé was my foster-brother. But I am forced to cry with the hounds!

124

A silence.

MOTHER MARIE. Forgive me if I ask for proof of your good intent.

THE COMMISSARY. I know your priest is hidden in the oasthouse.

MOTHER MARIE. I do not believe you.

THE COMMISSARY. He spoke to me.

MOTHER MARIE. What did he tell you?

THE COMMISSARY. That having climbed the wall of the nearby orchard, he was pursued by dogs, and forced to take refuge here once more. Do these precise details not convince you?

MOTHER MARIE. They only half convince me.

THE COMMISSARY. I will add then that a young nun has also been hidden there since yesterday morning, if what she says be true. She seemed to me to be dying of fright.

MOTHER MARIE. *(Without hiding anything more)* Then God be praised! It is surely Sister Blanche, and I did not know where to seek her. . . . I thank you for this piece of news, sir.

A silence. He glances about him.

THE COMMISSARY. I am taking with me the Commissaries and the patrol. Only the artisans will stay here until the evening. Beware of the blacksmith Blancard — he was brought up among the Benedictines of Restif and speaks the jargon of priests. He is a denouncer.

He goes off. The Commissaries talk together for several moments by the door. The conversation appears to be lively. Eventually they go off after having reassembled the patrol.

Scene XI

The screen now shows the sacked convent, though its invaders have gone. The last artisan to leave pauses for a moment on the threshold to take a final swig at his bottle, then throws it at the wall. A kind of door has been made by binding the broken planks together with wire.

125

Scene XII

The Community is now assembled in the Sacristy. The ladder and scaffolding which were used to bring down the convent bells can still be seen. Devastation. Straw and plaster everywhere. The grille in front of the choir is partly unfixed. A Sister keeps watch near the door. A few candles. The Chaplain's simple clothes are spotted with dirt and his shoes are covered in mud. A torn sleeve hangs down over his wrist, over a shirt which seems to be of very fine material and well-cared-for. A silence.

MOTHER MARIE. Speak to them, Father. For a long while they have been ready to take this step.

THE CHAPLAIN. It is not altogether within my ministry to do so, and I feel it would be more suitable, in the forced absence of her Reverence, if you yourself were to address the Community. My rôle will never be more than to receive and bless the vow you are about to pronounce, provided that it is spoken in full knowledge of the circumstances, freely and after due reflection.

Mother Marie's face reveals no opposition to this reply. Her attitude is always extremely simple and natural.

MOTHER MARIE. My sisters, a few words first of all. I know that some of you have been anxious since yesterday on behalf of our dear Sister Blanche. Mlle de la Force never left this house and it was she *(Sister Blanche starts, her face showing first a joyful surprise, then doubt, and finally anxiety)* who had the honor of being with the Chaplain, under circumstances which I cannot reveal, even if I thought it wise to do so, since I should thus risk compromising a friend, or at least a useful ally. That said, let us come to the purpose of our assembling here. I propose that we should pronounce together the vow of martyrdom in order to merit the continued existence of Carmel and the salvation of our fatherland.

There is no enthusiasm. The Sisters look at each other.

MOTHER MARIE. I find joy in seeing you receive this proposition as coldly as our Lord inspires me to make it. There is no question, in fact, of offering our poor lives with any great delusions on the score of their value, for the old saying which assures us that the manner of giving is worth more than the gift was never more true than it is today. We should give our lives with propriety. To give them with regret or at least with lurking thoughts of sadness cannot in any way offend against propriety. It would be, on the other hand, a grave and gross lack of propriety to inflame ourselves with long words and great gestures, like soldiers who take alcohol before the assault.

MOTHER JEANNE. To what exactly do we commit ourselves by this vow?

MOTHER MARIE. Not, certainly, to any kind of violent or indiscreet action which would be only provocation and defiance in the eyes of those who are capable enough of wreaking their vengeance on the innocent in our own persons. But there are legitimate means of avoiding martyrdom, and in advance we forbid ourselves the use of them, as a sick person refuses the medicine which would save him so that it may be used for others.

The aged Mother Jeanne discusses the matter for a moment with those near her.

MOTHER JEANNE. We perfectly approve your Reverence's explanations and cautions, but we fear they may be misunderstood by the youngest elements of this Community. The difficulty of these exceptional vows is the risk of their dividing the mind and even of their confliction with the conscience.

Mother Marie listens in silence. She does not hurry to reply.

MOTHER MARIE. That is why I have always held that the principle and the circumstances of such a vow should be recognized by all. The opposition of a single one of you will be enough for me to abandon the idea forthwith.

For some minutes Sister Constance has been looking, first surreptitiously and then openly, at Blanche de la Force. Blanche looks very tired. It should be ap-

parent that she will from now on be the plaything of circumstances, and that, in any case, she would never dare to oppose her companions in public.

MOTHER GÉRALD. *(Who is a little deaf, and in whose ear her neighbors have been whispering what has been said)* In such a case the oldest should speak for the youngest and in their name. Alas, there is more often shame than honor in wisdom at twenty.

MOTHER MARIE. My intention is that we should decide the matter by a secret vote. At least, the Chaplain will receive our responses in sacramental confidence.

Blanche's face clears visibly. Sister Constance keeps her eyes fixed on Blanche.

MOTHER MARIE. *(To the old nuns)* Does that give you satisfaction, my Mothers?

MOTHER GÉRALD. *(Having had the words repeated to her)* A great alleviation, at least.

THE CHAPLAIN. It will be best for you to pass in turn behind the altar.

The nuns rise. One group of young Sisters gathers together. One of them indicates Blanche with a discreet movement of her chin, and whispers.

SISTER ST. CHARLES. We can be sure there will be one voice against.

Sister Constance is quite near her. One cannot tell whether or not she has heard. She keeps her eyelids lowered. One by one the nuns disappear behind the altar and reappear almost immediately. It is imperative that all this should happen very quickly. When Blanche reappears her face is haggard (it could be that of a person who has just made up her mind by the toss of a coin). Constance now follows her with her eyes. The nuns sit again. The Chaplain approaches Mother Marie and speaks a few words to her in a low voice. Mother Marie states, still quite calmly:

MOTHER MARIE. There is a single vote in opposition. That is sufficient.

Sister Constance is as pale as death.

SISTER ST. CHARLES. *(Very softly)* We know who . . .
CONSTANCE. It was I.

General stupefaction. Blanche begins to weep, her head in her hands.

CONSTANCE. The Chaplain knows that I speak the truth. . . . But . . . but . . . I now declare myself in accordance with you all and . . . I . . . I wish . . . I should like you to permit me to pronounce the vow. . . . *(A silence)* I beg it of you in the name of God.
THE CHAPLAIN. I agree it shall be so. Rejoin your companions, Sister Constance. You will come here two by two. Sister Sacristan, open the book of the Holy Gospel and place it on the prie-dieu.

The Chaplain hastily puts on his vestments. Mother Marie places the book in the hands of a reader, who begins to read in a loud voice, recto tono, an extract from the Martyrology.

THE CHAPLAIN. The youngest first. Sister Blanche and Sister Constance, I pray you.

The contrast between the faces of Blanche and Constance is still striking. They kneel side by side and offer their lives to God for the salvation of Carmel and of France. At this moment sounds from the town should be heard: songs, passing feet — something of the sort — but very muffled. Blanche's voice is very distinct, but forced — it should be more or less obvious that she is exhausting her last resources. When she returns to her place at the back of the room, a confused noise is heard as the Sisters seek, following the wishes of the Chaplain, to group themselves according to age. Under cover of this hubbub, Sister Blanche is seen to leave the chapel and run off.

Scene XIII

The nuns are in lay attire and are leaving the convent, their bundles of clothes in their hands, During this time the pillage of the house continues. The Prioress returns meanwhile. She is first seen among her daughters, who are pressing round her. Spontaneously, without forethought, the Prioress asks:

THE PRIORESS. You are all here, my little daughters? Have I found you all again?

A few embarrassed looks. The Prioress does not press the point. She is obviously anxious to be alone with Mother Marie of the Incarnation. They are now seen alone.

THE PRIORESS. Finally you decided to pronounce this vow?

MOTHER MARIE. I had little hope of seeing you again, at least in this world. . . . Otherwise . . .

THE PRIORESS. Oh, I do not blame you! But I have always feared that you might be mistaken when generosity brought you to oppose the exaltation of evil with the exaltation of good, like two powerful voices trying to drown each other. It is when evil is at its height that we should take the least notice of it; such is the tradition and spirit of an Order like ours, devoted to contemplation. Yes, it is when the power of evil, which in any case is nothing but deception and illusion, reveals itself at its greatest that God becomes again the little Child in the manger, as if to escape His own justice and the demands of His own justice, and, so to speak, to cheat it. And if everything really happened as you have told me, is it not the sweet Childhood of our Lord, in the person of our poor little daughter Blanche, which may have to pay the price of this display of heroism? In thinking to assure our salvation, have we not compromised hers? Oh, I am only a poor nun, very much down-to-earth, and yet I have always been ready to believe that if strength is a virtue there is not enough of that virtue for everyone, that the strong are strong at the expense of the weak, and that finally weakness will be reconciled and glorified in the universal redemption. . . .

Mother Marie of the Incarnation has bowed her head. A long silence.

MOTHER MARIE. As soon as it be possible, I shall solicit your Reverence's permission to go and seek Mlle de la Force in Paris.

130

THE PRIORESS. I shall not refuse it you. *(A silence)* But it will cost me much to be alone at such a time.

Mother Marie slips to her knees before the Prioress.

MOTHER MARIE. I ask your Reverence's forgiveness for the sin I have committed. God grant that its expiation be hard enough that none shall suffer for it but I.

The Prioress blesses her and embraces her.

Part Five

Scene I

The Hôtel de la Force. The steps outside are deserted. A man arrives, a sans-culotte, wearing the cockade and the cap of Liberty. He enters the mansion (by the back staircase), goes to the drawing-room, and calls softly: "Mademoiselle Blanche!" No reply. The man is heard climbing the stairs.

Blanche's room. She hears her name, believes it to be her father, opens the door, and runs out. Seeing the man, she screams as she did at the beginning of the film. She flies back to her room and locks herself in. The man tries to reassure her by calling through the door: "Open the door! It is I, Antoine, your coachman. Your father has been arrested. We must go and secure his release."

Scene II

The Conciergerie prison. The interior of a cell, in which there are twenty or so prisoners. Disorder. Comings and goings of men who allow their great exhaustion to show as little as possible, and who are able still to brace themselves whenever necessary. An air-hole giving upon an inner court-yard, from which an incessant clamor is heard, which sometimes becomes louder to such an extent that it drowns the noise of conversations. Shouts, drum-rolls, foot-steps, the noise of carts. Nothing gives the impression of the discipline of a modern prison-camp. From time to time a revolutionary (of either sex) comes and crouches by the air-hole, presses his or her face against the bars, and hurls insults or makes jokes. A gaoler enters and calls:

THE GAOLER. The ci-devant Comte de Guiches.
A PRISONER. *(Ironically)* He is a Marquis, citoyen!
THE GAOLER. My paper says "Comte," not "Marquis."

A few prisoners stop talking in order to listen. Most of them continue their conversations.

A PRISONER. You are holding your paper upside-down, citoyen!
THE GAOLER. Bah! The clerk read the thing to me, and even if I cannot read, faith, I am not deaf!

The Marquis de Guiches had stretched out his hand to take the paper, but he now shrugs and says:

THE MARQUIS. Ah, you have always seemed to me to be a good fellow. So I will leave the matter to you.

He goes to a young woman who, on the gaoler's entry, broke off a game of cards and is now standing, smiling bravely.

THE MARQUIS. My dear Héloise, I pray you, keep these knick-knacks for me. I have tied them up in this handkerchief, and by my faith, they are all I have left in this world. I shall take into the next nothing but your good graces, my angel. *(A silence)* My young brother will laugh heartily. We have been wrangling for seven years over a hovel which is not worth five thousand livres, and now I leave everything to him. . . . It is true that I only do so because I am unable to retain anything for myself. . . . Farewell, Héloise. I would kiss your hand were it not that it would seem absurd. *(He speaks to the grey-haired prisoner, the young woman's partner, who has also ceased to play)* Gontran, you will give this good fellow an écu for me, and you will present my respects to the Marquis de la Force. I see he is sleeping over there and I would not dare wake him for so trivial a matter. *(To Héloise)* Farewell, my heart.

She stiffens visibly, but still bravely gives him her smile till the end, until he has passed through the door. Meanwhile the grey-haired prisoner has sat again.

GONTRAN. Will you deal?
HÉLOISE. No. I have no taste for the game this evening.
GONTRAN. As you wish.

He gathers the cards together and slips them in his pocket with a yawn. Héloise remains standing, very upright, her eyes downcast, but her head held high.

Gontran steps a few paces towards the fireplace, in front of which stands a young man whose hands are black with soot. The noise outside redoubles. Inside, the voices are raised accordingly. Comings and goings.

GONTRAN. Well, young man, and where have your exertions brought you?
THE YOUNG MAN. I have just prepared my work for tonight. Oh, if I had a better tool than this poor file we should be out of here this evening. But to wear out this old steel, groove by groove, is the very devil. . . .
GONTRAN. The devil is to give oneself so much trouble in order not to die.
THE YOUNG MAN. No — in order to live. Are you not all ashamed to let yourselves be killed without taking any action?
GONTRAN. And what would you have us do that would have any effect? To speak frankly, were there but one chance in a hundred of being dragged out of there by the feet, like a badger from its den, I should still prefer the tumbril a thousand times!
THE YOUNG MAN. The men of your generation have no love for life.
GONTRAN. We played with Life, and Life plays with you. We took Life, and Life takes you. You cling to Life as to a mistress who has never unclothed herself before your eyes.

134

ANOTHER GAOLER. The ci-devant Marquis de la Force.

The Marquis awakes. He takes a pinch of snuff and rises to his feet.

Scene III

The tribunal, between two wicket-gates. Interrogation of the Marquis.

ONE OF THE JUDGES. A man is here who has come to claim the ci-
devant in the name of his section.
A JUDGE. Let him enter.

The Coachman enters, holding the terrified Blanche by the hand.

THE COACHMAN. Citizen Judges, the young and attractive person
who accompanies me is the daughter of the ci-devant. The Republic
has just saved her from the hands of the priests, who had snatched her
from her old father to bury her for ever in the gaols of fanaticism and
superstition. . . . The little citoyenne comes to thank her protectors and
liberators.

The tribunal announces the liberation of Blanche and her father.

Scene IV

*The Hôtel de la Force. The big drawing room. The Marquis sits in an arm-
chair, whilst Blanche kneels beside him, her head buried in his lap. He comforts her. The Coachman acts the master of the house, and feasts his comrades
who have returned to the mansion with the Marquis and his daughter.*

Scene V

Compiègne. The assembled Carmelites in lay clothes face the Municipal officers.

ONE OF THE OFFICERS. Citoyennes, we congratulate you on your discipline and your good citizenship. But we warn you that the Nation will watch you with care henceforth. No Community life, no relations with the enemies of the Republic, nor with refractory priests, the tools of the Pope and the Tyrants. In ten minutes' time you will go one by one to the office to collect the certificate which enables you to enjoy once more the benefits of liberty under the surveillance and protection of the Law.

He goes out. The Sisters, who were standing in two rows, form groups among themselves. The Prioress and Mother Marie remain alone, away from the others. The Prioress beckons to one of the nuns, an old religious who, in her lay clothes, could not be distinguished from any other poor woman.

THE PRIORESS. Sister Gérald, it is essential that the priest should be warned. We have agreed that he should celebrate Mass today, and I see now that there will be too much danger both for him and for us.

Mother Gérald goes out. A silence.

THE PRIORESS. Do you not think so, Mother Marie?
MOTHER MARIE. I place my trust in you for what I may henceforth think or not think, but if I was wrong to act as I did, the fact is still that what is done is done. How can we reconcile the spirit of our vow with this prudence?
THE PRIORESS. Each one of you will answer for her vow before God, but it is I who must answer for all of you, and I am old enough to know how to keep my accounts in order.

Scene VI

The scene changes. The priest is seen returning with Mother Gérald. He goes up to the Prioress. As he reaches her he turns and blesses the nuns, who all kneel together.

Scene VII

The scene changes again. The Chaplain is now alone with the Prioress and Mother Marie of the Incarnation in a small room.

THE CHAPLAIN. Yes, the Marquis de la Force has indeed been guillotined. My information is trustworthy.

THE PRIORESS. What can we do for Blanche?

THE CHAPLAIN. I should have liked to conceal her in the country for some time, so that she could gather her strength; but the poor child is in no condition to support me in such an enterprise. From what my niece tells me, the guards in the mansion treat her as a servant and she is under their surveillance day and night. Sooner or later she will meet her father's fate. We shall not succeed in saving her life, but perhaps we shall preserve her from a wretched death. She must be brought back to Compiègne.

MOTHER MARIE. With her Reverence's permission, I will go to seek her and bring her back.

THE CHAPLAIN. Here is a note for my niece, Rose Ducor, the actress. She is a good girl, in whom we may have confidence and who knows all the circumstances. If you succeed in taking Blanche to her home, the most difficult part will have been achieved. I shall try to rejoin you there.

Scene VIII

The Hôtel de la Force. In a room on the first floor, Blanche is crouching by the hearth, cooking. The door below is heard to open, footsteps mount the staircase, a woman's voice calls, and a knock comes at the door. Blanche

137

goes to the mantelpiece on tiptoe, takes a key, crosses the room, and goes out by the door opposite to the one on which someone has knocked. Passing through two or three small rooms, she half-opens a door which allows her to see who is there without herself being seen. She recognizes Mother Marie of the Incarnation and opens the door wide. Mother Marie starts at the sound. They both enter by the door on which Marie knocked into the room where Blanche was cooking.

BLANCHE. It is you. . . . (*She looks at Mother Marie with a strange expression of humble affection mingled with distrust*)

MOTHER MARIE. Yes. I came to find you. It is time.

BLANCHE. I am not free to follow you now. . . . But in a little while . . . perhaps . . .

MOTHER MARIE. Not in a little while, but straightway. In a few days it will be too late.

BLANCHE. Too late for what?

Mother Marie shudders. It is apparent that this beginning to the conversation disappoints and disconcerts her.

MOTHER MARIE. For your safety.

BLANCHE. My safety. . . . (*Silence*) Are you going to tell me that I shall be safe there?

MOTHER MARIE. You will run fewer risks there than here, Blanche.

BLANCHE. I cannot believe you. In times like these, is there any other security than mine? Where I am, who would think of looking for me? Death strikes only above me. . . . But I feel so tired, Mother Marie! (*She shivers*) See, my stew is burning! It is your fault! (*She kneels by the fire and raises the cover of the saucepan*) Alas! Alas! What will become of me?

Mother Marie has also knelt, and she quickly pours the stew into another saucepan. Then she covers the fire with ashes and puts the saucepan over it again, after having smelt the stew.

MOTHER MARIE. Do not torment yourself, Blanche. Look! The harm has been repaired.

Blanche sobs.

MOTHER MARIE. Why do you weep?

BLANCHE. I weep because you are so good. But I am ashamed, too, to weep. I wish everyone would leave me in peace and never think of me again. *(With a sudden violence)* What do they reproach me with? What have I done? I do not offend against God. Fear does not offend against God. I was born in fear, I have lived in it, I still live in it, and as everyone despises fear it is right that I should live also in contempt. That I have believed for a long while. The only person who could have stopped me saying it was my father. He is dead. They guillotined him a few days ago. *(She twists her hands)* In his own house what other rôle should I have, I who am so unworthy of him and of his name, than that of a wretched servant? Only yesterday they beat me. . . . *(With a kind of defiance)* Yes, they beat me.

A silence.

MOTHER MARIE. The misfortune, my daughter, is not to be despised but to despise oneself.

Another silence. Then, in a firm yet very simple, very even voice, Mother Marie speaks:

MOTHER MARIE. Sister Blanche of the Agony of Christ?

On Mother Marie's words, Blanche rises, as if despite herself, and stands facing her, her eyes dry.

BLANCHE. Yes, Mother?

MOTHER MARIE. I am going to give you an address. Remember it well. Mlle Rose Ducor, 2 Rue St. Denis. This person has been warned. You will be safe with her. . . . 2 Rue St. Denis. *(A pause)* I shall wait for you there until tomorrow evening.

BLANCHE. I shall not come. I cannot come there.

MOTHER MARIE. You will come. I know that you will come, my Sister.

At this moment the voice of one of the guards is heard calling Blanche for some errand. Blanche runs off and leaves Mother Marie, who slips away.

Scene IX

Blanche is seen in the street. She carries a little basket filled with shopping. The street is busy. A great noise drawing nearer. The Ça Ira. The passers-by begin to disperse hither and thither. A troop of sans-culottes rushes by, armed with pikes and sabres and followed by a man carrying a pike on which a human head is impaled. Five or six passers-by, including Blanche, have only time to fling themselves into a carriage gateway, the door of which they close. They find themselves in a little courtyard. The noise in the street increases. The sheltering passers-by look at each other at first with distrust. There are two old women, a very young girl, an old gentleman who is poorly clad but who has something of the ci-devant about him, and a young man who, having glanced around, scrambles over a wall and disappears. Those who remain seem gradually to become reassured. Blanche remains aloof. One of the old women speaks:

FIRST OLD WOMAN. If you ask me, we are not yet at the end of our troubles.

THE OLD GENTLEMAN. Indeed, life in Paris is becoming increasingly difficult.

SECOND OLD WOMAN. Oh, it is no better anywhere else, sir.

FIRST OLD WOMAN. If it is not worse. I come from Nanterre. . . .

SECOND OLD WOMAN. And I from Compiègne.

Blanche starts. It is evident that she is struggling with her fear. She speaks in a faint voice:

BLANCHE. You come from Compiègne?

SECOND OLD WOMAN. Yes, my pretty. I came from there yesterday with a cartload of vegetables. There are some wicked rascals there — a score or so — who are all afraid of each other and who, to puff themselves up, make enough commotion for six hundred. The day before yesterday they arrested the nuns of the Carmel. *(She notices Blanche's shocked expression and goes on)* Perhaps you have relations there?

BLANCHE. Oh no, madame. And I have never been to Compiègne either. I arrived in Paris with my employers only eight days ago, from Roche-sur-Yon.

She forces herself to control the nervous trembling which has overtaken her. Her face shows her terror and also something which resembles a desperate resolution. Quickly summoning her courage, she slips out. The old gentleman is sitting on a bench, holding a pinch of snuff between his fingers. The two old women look at each other, nodding their heads.

FIRST OLD WOMAN. Queer kind of servant, m'dear.

Scene X

Blanche arrives at Rose Ducor's home. She is out of breath and nearly out of her wits. She sits on a chair, her head in her hands. She repeats:

BLANCHE. They must be saved! They must not be killed! They must be saved, whatever the cost! My God! My God! They must not be killed!

Rose Ducor and Mother Marie hurry to her.

MOTHER MARIE. What do you mean?

BLANCHE. *(In a broken voice, in which, nevertheless, a new revolt and horror can already be distinguished)* I was shopping in the market . . . as every morning when . . . when an old woman told me . . .

MOTHER MARIE. Our Sisters are in prison?

BLANCHE. Yes.

MOTHER MARIE. *(With great feeling)* God be praised!

Silence. Mother Marie's lips move; she is praying. Blanche's head is still in her hands. At Mother Marie's "God be praised" she did, however, shudder. Mother Marie touches her shoulder.

MOTHER MARIE. Sister Blanche, we must go to Compiègne.

Blanche raises her head.

BLANCHE. That is true. . . . Oh, Mother Marie, if there is any way of
saving them, it seems to me that this time I should have the courage.

MOTHER MARIE. There is no question of saving them, but only of fulfilling with them the vow which we freely made so few days ago.

BLANCHE. What! We shall let them die without attempting anything to
save them?

MOTHER MARIE. What matters, my daughter, is that we should not let
them die without us.

BLANCHE. What need have they of us in death?

MOTHER MARIE. Is it a daughter of Carmel who speaks thus?

BLANCHE. Die! Die! You no longer have any word on your lips but
that. Will you never grow weary of killing and dying? Will you never
tire of the blood of others or of your own blood?

MOTHER MARIE. There is no horror except in crime, my daughter, and
it is by the sacrifice of innocent lives that that horror is effaced, the
crime itself restored within the order of divine charity. . . .

Blanche stamps her foot.

BLANCHE. I do not want them to die! And I do not want to die!

*She runs out before Mother Marie can stop her. In the street doorway she
falls into the arms of the refractory priest, who cries out for joy:*

THE CHAPLAIN. Dear Sister Blanche, you are here! God be praised!

*But Blanche, quite beyond herself, looks wildly at the priest, pulls away
from him roughly, and disappears.*

Scene XI

THE CHAPLAIN. What was the matter with Sister Blanche?
MOTHER MARIE. You saw her?
THE CHAPLAIN. She showed an extraordinary agitation. She ran off without saying a word to me.

Mother Marie smiles.

MOTHER MARIE. She is in revolt again, like some naughty child. But what matter! Nothing now can wrest her from the sweet pity of Jesus Christ. *(A pause)* So I shall leave for Compiègne alone.

The Priest is silent.

MOTHER MARIE. Do you disapprove of my doing so?
THE CHAPLAIN. No. I merely think that it would be wiser to wait until we are better informed of what is happening. Your Sisters are prisoners, I know. But it is in no way certain that they are condemned. May not your intervention risk aggravating their position?
MOTHER MARIE. Again, Father, I ask what will remain of our vow of martyrdom if we always act with this prudence?
THE CHAPLAIN. My Mother, you pronounced that vow in a spirit of obedience, and it is in a spirit of obedience that you should fulfill it. Write to your Prioress and ask her what you should do.

Scene XII

The prison. Morning, but it is still very dark. Some of the Sisters are sitting with their backs to the walls. The Little King of Glory has been placed on a rickety table. Some faded flowers in a broken pot. On the table is a white handkerchief, which is too small for it. A single cheap half-burnt candle. In the dim light the nuns come and kneel in twos or threes before the statue. Sighs can be heard, which might equally be stifled sobs. Several Sisters cough. It is cold. The anguish of dawn. A little apart, in the corner of the room, to the right of the table, the Prioress is lying. Sister Constance, who has just knelt before the Little King of Glory, cries out in pain as she rises.

SISTER VALENTINE OF THE CROSS. What is the matter, Sister Constance?

CONSTANCE. I went to sleep beneath the skylight, and now I have a crick. My poor neck. . . . *(She rubs it with both hands, laughing)*

SISTER ST. CHARLES. *(With a start)* Oh, Sister Constance!

SISTER ALICE. If your nerves are in such good condition, why torment those of others?

Sister Constance suddenly realizes what she has said, and shudders in her turn. . . .

CONSTANCE. In faith, I . . . I . . .

SISTER MARTHE. *(Cutting her short, in a rather forced voice)* I have not slept at all. *(Lower)* Our poor old Mother Gérald snored the night through.

SISTER GERTRUDE. It is her catarrh. I know it well. My cell was near hers.

Sister Marthe sobs.

SISTER FÉLICITÉ. Why do you weep, Sister Marthe?

SISTER ST. CHARLES. *(More and more hysterically)* Why . . . ? Why . . . ? And why then do you say "my cell was"? Why speak of our dear House as if we shall never see it again?

The Prioress has just clapped her hands softly. The religious gather round her. The day is hardly beginning.

THE PRIORESS. My daughters, now our first night in prison is ending. It was the most difficult. We have come to the end of it, nevertheless. The next will find us quite accustomed to our new condition, which is, in any case, not new to us; it is not, in fact, more than a change of surroundings. None can rob us of a freedom which we have cast off so long ago.

144

SISTER CLAIRE. It is to God that our freedom belongs, but your Reverence is still its guardian by virtue of the charge which we have laid upon her voluntarily and freely.

THE PRIORESS. What do you mean, Sister Claire?

SISTER CLAIRE. I mean that even in casting off her own freedom, your Reverence still retains the charge and the disposal of our freedom, and that she cannot then leave our fates entirely to God.

OTHER OLD SISTERS. True . . . true. . . .

Murmurs from the younger Sisters.

SISTER CLAIRE. My little Sisters, it is possible that at your age obedience still seems a soft pillow on which one has only to lay one's head. But we know that obedience, for all it seems so different from command, is also a burden. Yes, my little daughters, it is as difficult to learn to obey as to command. To obey is not to allow oneself to be led passively, as a blind man follows his dog. An old nun like myself wishes no more than to die in obedience, but in an active and conscious obedience. Although we agree that we possess nothing in this world, it is, nevertheless, true that our death is our own death — no one can die in my place.

SISTER ST. CHARLES. *(Who can restrain herself no longer)* Must we always listen to talk of death? Why death? Are we not innocent?

CONSTANCE. Be quiet, Sister St. Charles. . . .

SISTER MATHILDE. Are we even so sure of being sacrificed through hatred of our faith? Shall we not be paying for the sins of others?

SISTER ST. CHARLES. She is right. What have we to do with all these politics?

THE PRIORESS. Peace, my daughters! Let me first reply to Sister Claire. I know I shall have charge of you all to the end, my daughter. I do not think to delude myself on that score.

SISTER CLAIRE. Is it your Reverence's intention to speak alone on our behalf before the Tribunal? And if not so, to what lengths can we go without contravening the spirit of the vow we have made?

SISTER ANNE. Yes. Shall we have the right to defend ourselves? Shall we be condemned without having been heard?

SISTER VALENTINE OF THE CROSS. Should not we be ashamed to dispute our poor lives with the assassins of priests and the pillagers of churches?

THE PRIORESS. *(Raising her voice a little)* There is no shame in justifying oneself, even before judges who are without faith. The innocent person who justifies himself lends more testimony to the truth than to himself. . . . *(She stops for a moment. Silence. She is seen to be praying)* My daughters, it was in my absence that you pronounced this vow of martyrdom. But whether or not it was timely, God would not now allow so generous an act to serve only to disturb your consciences. Well, I assume that vow. I am henceforth responsible before the Divine Majesty. I am and shall be, whatever happens, the sole judge of its fulfillment. Yes, I accept its burden and leave you its merit since I have not pronounced it myself. Do not then disturb yourselves over it any more, my daughters. I have always answered for you in this world, and I am in no mood today to feel my responsibility discharged in any respect. Be calm! I shall do my all for your lives and your souls, and at this moment when more than ever I feel myself your mother, both are almost equally precious to me. If I am wrong, God will pardon me. The mothers of the holy martyrs, after all, appear but rarely in the calendar of saints.

A young Sister, who was holding her head in her hands, comes forward and kneels to kiss her Reverence's hand. The tears are still running down her face, which now shows a naive, childlike confidence.

SISTER GERTRUDE. While we are with your Reverence, we shall never fear anything.

Other Sisters approach. One of the old nuns says:

MOTHER JEANNE. Will your Reverence deign to give us your benediction?

They all kneel. Then conversations start up again in an entirely different key from before. An almost joyful sound.

CONSTANCE. And what has become of Sister Blanche?

THE PRIORESS. *(Who has overheard)* I know no more of her than you, my little one.

CONSTANCE. She will come back.

SISTER ST. CHARLES. Why are you so sure, Sister Constance?

CONSTANCE. Because . . . *(She stops, disconcerted)* Because . . . *(Then very confused, but incapable of going back on what she has said)* Because of a dream I had.

Laughter.

SISTER FÉLICITÉ. Reverend Mother, do you think we shall be tried to-day?

THE PRIORESS. I know not.

SISTER ST. CHARLES. *(Very naïvely)* Are they going to interrogate us one by one? Will it last a long time?

SISTER ALICE. And will . . . will they let us . . . let us confess?

Sister Constance, pointing out a young Sister who has suddenly paled and put her head in her hands, places her finger on her lips.

SISTER ST. CHARLES. *(Shrugging her shoulders)* Bah! We are not weak little girls, after all. In faith, if the Chaplain may only be on our path, I shall not ask more.

THE PRIORESS. Come, come, my daughters, leave these imaginings there; none of it is happening this very moment. . . . I quite believe that the youngest among you will escape without harm. If these people are not monsters or if they know anything of our Holy Rule, whom can they attack but me?

SEVERAL VOICES. Oh, nothing will ever part us from your Reverence.

SISTER CLAIRE. God knows I would not willingly change my fate for that of our Mother Marie of the Incarnation or that of our Sister Blanche.

MOTHER GÉRALD. Alas! They must have been arrested too. . . .

SISTER CLAIRE. Exactly. . . . How can we think to complain when we are united here together . . . ! How they must envy us! Must they not consider their misfortune greater than ours?

147

Scene XIII

The Tribunal pronounces the condemnation to death of the sixteen Carmelites (including Mother Marie of the Incarnation, condemned in contumacy) "for having conducted anti-revolutionary conventicles, engaged in fanatical activities, and preserved anti-libertarian writings."

Scene XIV

The Carmelites assemble in a little inner courtyard. The Prioress speaks:

THE PRIORESS. My daughters, I wished with all my heart to save you. . . . Yes, I would have had the chalice withdrawn from your lips, for I have loved you since the first day, as it is a mother's nature to do; and what mother makes the sacrifice of her children, even to the Divine Majesty, with good grace? If I have acted wrongly, God will be merciful. I am such that you are my endowment, and I am not one of those who squander their endowments. But when all is said and done, what does it matter, my daughters? We have come to the end; death is all that remains. Blessed be the God who makes the torment that we are about to suffer like a last office of our dear Community! My children, the hour has come to remind you of the vow you have pronounced. Until this moment I wished to answer for it alone. Henceforth I can assume only that part of it which falls to me by right, and yet I should humbly claim it in the name of our admirable Mother Marie of the Incarnation, for it is her share that is now mine, unworthy though I am. My daughters, I place you solemnly under obedience — for the last time, once for all — with my maternal benediction.

Scene XV

Rose Ducor arrives in her rooms, takes from under her cloak the statue of the Little King of Glory, and places it on a table. Mother Marie of the Incarnation kneels to venerate it.

148

Scene XVI

Rose Ducor's house. The Chaplain arrives, overcome by emotion.

THE CHAPLAIN. They are condemned to death.
MOTHER MARIE. All of them?
THE CHAPLAIN. All of them!
MOTHER MARIE. God! *(A silence)* And . . .
THE CHAPLAIN. It will be today no doubt, or tomorrow. . . . What are you doing, Mother Marie?
MOTHER MARIE. I cannot let them die without me!
THE CHAPLAIN. Of what importance is your will in this matter? God chooses or holds back whom He pleases.
MOTHER MARIE. I made the vow of martyrdom. . . .
THE CHAPLAIN. It was to God that you made it. It is to Him that you must answer for it, and not to your Sisters. If it pleases God to relieve you of it, He takes back only that which belongs to Him.
MOTHER MARIE. This is dishonor!
THE CHAPLAIN. That is the word I expected to hear. Oh, I do not condemn it. With you it is indeed the cry of nature in agony. That is the blood, yes, that is the blood which God asks of you, and which you must shed. You would have given joyfully the blood which flows in your veins, you would have shed it like water. But each drop of this kind costs you more than your life.

Mother Marie of the Incarnation remains standing in the attitude of one who gathers her strength to resist an almost unbearable torture.

MOTHER MARIE. In vain will they look for me in their last moment.
THE CHAPLAIN. Think only of another look, on which you should fix your eyes.

Scene XVII

The Place de la Revolution. The Carmelites climb down from the tumbril at the foot of the scaffold. In the front rank of the thick crowd, wearing a cap of Liberty, the priest can be recognized. He murmurs the absolution, makes a furtive sign of the cross, and quickly disappears. Immediately the Sisters chant the Salve Regina, then the Veni Creator. Their voices are clear and very firm. The crowd, gripped, is silent. Only the base of the scaffold is visible. One by one the Sisters mount it, still singing, but as they disappear the volume of sound decreases. Only two voices; only one. But at this moment, in another part of the large square, a new voice is raised, crisper, more resolute than the others, yet with something childlike about it. And towards the scaffold, through the crowd which, astounded, makes room, one sees approaching the slight figure of Blanche de la Force. Her face seems stripped of all fear.

> *Deo Patri sit gloria*
> *Et Filio qui a mortuis*
> *Surrexit ac Paraclito*
> *In sæculorum sæcula*

A sudden movement of the crowd. A group of women surround Blanche and push her towards the scaffold. She is lost to sight. And suddenly her voice is no longer heard, just as one by one the voices of her Sisters ceased.

The End